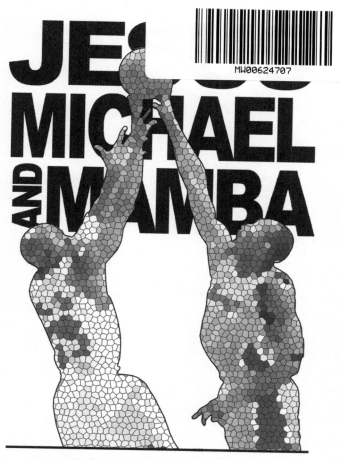

JESUS MICHAEL AND MAMBA

Spiritual Growth for
Hoopers & Sneakerheads

JOHN TETER AND
MICHAEL THOMAS

Published in 2021 by Antioch Creative
Long Beach, CA
FolAntioch.org

Design by Cindy Kiple

Unless otherwise noted, Scripture quotations are taken from the English Standard Version Bible.

Title: *Jesus, Michael & Mamba*

Names: John Teter, Michael Thomas

Publisher: Antioch Creative

Description: First paperback edition - including acknowledgment references

Identifiers: ISBN 978-1-7377135-0-0 (softcover)

Subjects: Spirituality; Sports

For Eric Puckett
Thank you for mentoring me in my early years in the
faith & deepening my love for the game.
Michael

For Isaac Flores
How can I ever thank you enough for Section 308?
John

CONTENTS

INTRODUCTION

ON YOUR FEET

JESUS, MICHAEL & MAMBA?

Jesus of Nazareth, Michael Jordan of Wilmington, North Carolina, and Kobe Bryant of Lower Merion, Pennsylvania.

Really?

God come to earth, Air Jordan, and the Black Mamba?

Yes!

Why would two pastors write about the Living God and two of the greatest to ever lace them up?

The answer is right there in the **Bible**. (Note: When you come a cross a bolded word, it is important to the Christian faith and has a teaching note in the Glossary at the end of the book).

Many authors of Scripture looked to images of the day to describe the life of faith. Jesus taught in parables to break it way down for everybody. As Bible teachers, we love connecting current culture to timeless truth. One passage challenges us to live out our faith like an athlete or we won't receive the ultimate crown of glory. This teaching is found in 2 Timothy 2:5 (**chapter and verse**). We think it is time to make this passage come alive. And who did it better than Michael Jordan and Kobe Bryant? These two NBA Hall of Famers mastered the fundamentals, conquered the global sports landscape, and created a legacy that will last generations.

We are here to connect some of the dots to help us not only understand Jordan and Bryant the basketball players, but to spotlight their unique gifts, drive and accomplishments as we consider our own growth. Our research and personal illustrations will provide a road map for your faith, no matter where you are coming from. The timing for this project is important, as Kobe Bryant's untimely passing, Michael Jordan's 'The Last Dance' documentary, and Jordan recently escorting Bryant into the NBA Hall of Fame, dominated the beginning of our new decade.

JANUARY 26, 2020

That overcast Sunday began like every other Sunday. At the end of our weekly Sunday worship service, I (John) packed my Bible and preaching folder into my Kobe Bryant backpack. Suddenly, Isaac Flores grabbed my arm. Isaac and I have been dear friends since high school. He is also a twenty-eight year veteran of the Los Angeles Lakers Band. With shock and disbelief on his face, he showed me the headline on his phone: 'Kobe Bryant Dead in Helicopter Accident.'

I was stunned, shocked and could barely mouth the words: "Ike, Kobe can't be dead."

As a lifelong Lakers fan, it was so much to process. The Lakers legend, husband, father, Academy Award winner, and champion of youth sports, was just getting started. In so many ways he was becoming the version of himself he was supposed to be, leaving behind the missteps of his youth. At 42, his whole life was ahead of him.

I looked around the church auditorium. Our energetic young church, typically filled with laughter and loud conversation after service, was eerily silent. People spoke in hushed tones as they also scrolled in disbelief.

Later that day along with my wife Becky and our children I watched the news reports with tears in our eyes. We are a diehard Laker family. When we began dating, Becky bought tickets for my birthday and took me to my first Lakers game at the Fabulous Forum. Our families have celebrated so many moments of Kobe's career, filled with all the joy he brought our family and our city. And in a moment everything changed as we watched the images of the helicopter crash site and billowing smoke.

The sharp pain I felt at losing Kobe transported me back to my childhood anguish. When I was ten years old, I lost my father to a glider plane accident. Even forty years later, this sudden and severe soul wound is still very present. One moment my father's vessel was in the air, and just like Kobe's, the next moment it crashed to the ground. I immediately thought of the surviving Bryant children. Their lives would never be the same.

FEBRUARY 24, 2020

The Bryant family and the Los Angeles Lakers waited one month for Kobe and Gigi Bryant's 'Celebration of Life.' They chose February 24 because the date honored both Bryants. Kobe wore number 24. Gigi, a prep phenom with a clear path to star in the WNBA, wore number 2. February 24 combined both of their numbers (2/24). Numbers are a real big deal in the Bible. We loved the poetic design in the date.

For over a month, the city of Los Angeles had poured out their love, sorrow and prayers for Kobe, Gigi and the Bryant family. Mourners created a seemingly endless shrine spanning four blocks across the street from Staples Center. For two straight weeks, fans brought flowers, paintings, photographs, and even laid down their Black Mamba sneakers to honor their fallen hero. Tickets for the memorial event at Staples Center sold out in minutes.

At the memorial, Beyoncé and Christina Aguilera sang Kobe's favorite songs. Alicia Keys performed a breathtaking rendition of Beethoven's 'Moonlight Sonata.' Vanessa Bryant, with incredible strength and poise, eulogized her husband. Kobe's best friend and current Lakers general manager, Rob Pelinka, reflected on Kobe as a parent and his great love for his daughters.

Shaquille O'Neal told jokes and stories that touched everyone's heart. But Michael Jordan took the stage to share things many had never heard before.

Very little had been written about their relationship beyond their infamous, and very awkward, first interaction. Michael Jordan, now retired, returned to the United Center for a Bulls-Lakers game. In his book *Three Ring Circus*, Jeff Pearlman shares the story of Kobe and

Jordan's first meeting. After the game Coach Phil Jackson arranged a meeting between Kobe and his idol. "Michael's back there smoking a cigar," Jackson recalled. "And Kobe comes in and the first thing he says-the very first thing-is 'I can take you one-on-one.' It wasn't said jokingly. And Michael said, 'You probably can. You're 22 and I'm 36.' It was weird." Because of that interaction, reports were that Kobe received a cold shoulder from Jordan in the early years. But Kobe grew on Jordan.

At the podium that afternoon, 'Crying Jordan' stood with tears streaming down his face. He spoke of late night texts, secret meetings, and his role as Kobe's big brother. "When Kobe Bryant died, a piece of me died," said the great Air Jordan. "As I look in this arena, and across the globe, a piece of you died or else you wouldn't be here."

After watching the 'Celebration of Life' I called Pastor Michael Thomas. He is my dear friend and brother and the biggest Michael Jordan fan I know. I am the biggest Kobe Bryant fan he knows. We talked about their friendship and what each meant to generations of basketball fans. As we spoke, suddenly an idea popped into our minds. What if we collaborated on a book about the many spiritual insights we learned from MJ and Mamba?

We pulled up out a blank page and began to jot down **core issues** that inspire and inform us: family, work ethic, loss and legacy were at the top of our long list. We began to believe in our spirits that God wanted us to study the lives of Jordan and Bryant so that we might connect their immense influence to the One who has eternal influence. What you have in your hand is a book. But we also like to think of it as a bridge. And we are inviting you to journey with us through the very thin spiritual veil and into the next dimension where Jesus lives, moves andhas His being.

INTRODUCTIONS

For 15 years the following introduction went down before every Chicago Bulls game, first at Chicago Stadium, and then at The United Center. The visiting team has already been introduced. The arena goes dark. The drama begins to form like a wave in the crowd.

The music starts. The video montage drops. Lasers cut across the arena. The fans go wild. And then Ray Clay, the Chicago Bulls public address announcer, brings the crowd to a frenzy as he introduces the Bulls last starter:

From North Carolina
At Guard
6 foot 6 inches
Michael Jordan

For 20 years the following went down before every home Los Angeles Lakers game at The Fabulous Forum and then Staples Center. The visiting team has already been introduced. The arena goes dark. The drama begins to form like a wave in the crowd. The music starts. The video montage drops. Lasers cut across the arena. The fans go wild. And then, Lawrence Tanter, the Los Angeles Lakers public address announcer, brings the Lakers faithful to a frenzy as he introduces the Lakers last starter:

Number 24 on the floor
6 foot 6 inches
Guard
From Lower Merion High School
Kobe Bryant

While there is significantly less drama in our introductions, we wanted you to get know us a little before we meet at half-court and the ball is thrown in the air.

We are not just **pastors**. We are fans. We love this game. And we love Michael Jordan and Kobe Bryant. We are both pastors of **multi-ethnic churches**. With our families, each of us started our churches. And we are not just pastors and fans. We are also **apostles**. Every church had to start sometime and we both planted new churches in Seattle and Long Beach. Our cities (Los Angeles and Seattle) are full of cultural, racial, economic, and even religious division. And we have dedicated our lives to following God, bringing people to God and keeping people together in the love of God. We also are working hard to make sure we don't come off too religious for you, especially if you are new to the faith. We are so glad you are checking Jesus out by reading this book!

PASTOR MICHAEL THOMAS

I (PMT) will never forget the time a church leader rebuked our senior pastor and me (the youth pastor) because we were not wearing our '**Sunday best.**' At the time, my pastor and I were 25 and 24 years old, respectively, and we were both wearing athletic jogging suits…in the church! This particular leader expected us to lead, live—and probably sleep—in a 3-piece suit. What he didn't understand was that our love for athletics and the church were both deep parts of our DNA. Where he saw an expectation to separate the two, we were convinced that they were connected. In other words, I have to be authentically who I am. Sports and spirituality have a lot in common. We don't need to separate them, we need to explore how sports can inspire our faith life, and help us to run in such a way that we not only finish the race, but also finish it well.

I had the great joy and privilege to be born and raised on the South Side of Chicago. Although my family currently lives in Seattle—the greatest city in the world (sorry, not sorry, John). I cannot tell you how awesome it is to be from Chicago and to have grown up in the 'Windy City' during the 90s. Michael Jordan literally lit our city on fire every spring. It was truly incredible!

There was no greater feeling than to be 11 years old in 1988 when your city hosts the NBA All-Star weekend and to witness Michael Jordan dunk from the free-throw line wearing the 3s. I remember not only the 6 championships but the feeling that his trophies brought to our city. With MJ leading the Bulls, we always knew that even if there was a half of a second left on the clock, Jordan would somehow win us the game! Because Michael was great, our city was great! And if Chicago was great, it made me and every person from Chicago feel great too. His passion to win, commitment to preparation, and unwavering focus continues to inspire me in my faith journey and approach to service.

In one season of my life, the Jordan family attended the same church I grew up in. I remember feeling even someone as great as Michael Jordan recognized that he needed someone greater. All of the awards, fame and money did not fulfill his soul. He came to worship Jesus, the One who is the way, the truth and the life!

JOHN TETER

I (JT) was born and raised in Los Angeles. When I was nine, I watched my first Laker games on a black and white television. Magic Johnson was in his first year, and I thought every point guard had a triple double every night. As a die-hard Lakers fan, I was 26 years old when the Lakers traded with the Charlotte Hornets to roster a kid named Kobe. For 20 years, I watched Kobe Bryant grow up right before my eyes, master his craft, and go on to conquer the NBA.

Did you know that the Los Angeles Lakers were the first team in the NBA to have a live band perform at every home game? When Dr. Jerry Buss bought the Lakers in 1979, the NBA was not popular. Magic Johnson's first NBA finals, against Dr. J and the 76ers was broadcast on tape delay. Yes, the NBA finals would be shown hours after the games were finished after the local news. People were just not that into hoops. Dr. Buss was a loyal Trojan and saw 100,000 people pour into the Los Angeles Memorial Coliseum every other Saturday to cheer on the national champion Trojans. So he set out to make the Lakers experience more like USC football. He brought in cheerleaders and many gifted musicians of the USC marching band to form the 'Laker Band.' If you visit Staples Center today, there is one section that is different from all of the others. Section 308 was built for the Laker Band. Five rows of seats were eliminated to provide the band a performance platform. Isaac Flores has been in the Laker Band since 1992. Carrying his trombone case to Lakers games and bonding with the band has brought great joy to my life. My love for the Lakers, and Kobe, runs deep.

HOW THE BOOK IS ORGANIZED

In the chapters ahead, you will experience a blend of Jordan, Bryant and Jesus. The insights into our basketball heroes are from biographies we have read, documentaries and interviews we have consumed, and personal experiences. The chapters are designed around the concept of the core issues. We believe there are at least seven central issues that each of us, like Jordan and Bryant, must navigate in our lives. Here is our list of core issues that we will be addressing:

1. Foundations
2. Destiny
3. Drive
4. Teachers
5. Race
6. Loss
7. Legacy

For those who seek Him, the risen, reigning and soon to return Jesus of Nazareth is found in the **Bible**. For those of you who are new to faith, no man ever spoke like Jesus. He proclaimed that He not only was with God before the earth was created, but that He was God (John 1:1). He taught that His words are Spirit and life so if you want to find him, you know where to look (John 6:63). And He even declared that if we see Him, we have seen the Father (John 14:9). This reveals to us that if we want to know God, we need to spend time in the Bible. He is found in the sacred pages of Scripture, not mainstream media, social media or any other secondary source.

In the chapters ahead, we want to serve as your Biblical translators. For some of us, opening the Bible can be so intimidating. Many Bibles are physically big, hard to understand, and people who just don't know might think of it as leftovers from an ancient time. We ask you to think of us as your guides as you navigate new spiritual territory. We believe that the Bible is an icon just like the ones of your desk top or your phone. If it is untouched it will just sit there and just take up screen space. But if it is opened, it can open up to you a whole new world. We have seen that new world. And it is beautiful. We are eager to share with you what we have experienced.

In each chapter, we have not only highlighted the core issue, but also provide a connected Bible teaching. We have chosen to use the ESV **translation** of the Bible. We like to joke that this is the 'Extra Saucy Version' or 'Especially Spiritual Version.' It actually stands for English Standard Version. It is a strong translation produced by many who have dedicated their lives to mastering the Hebrew and Greek languages to most accurately translate the original documents into our language.

We provide enough background for you to be comfortable, but not too much to overwhelm you. If you want to do a deeper dive, religious words and concepts are in bold. There is a glossary in the back for every highlighted word to help you grow in your understanding. For example, the word **grace** is used so often in Christian circles, but many don't stop to think what the word really means. The glossary provides a clear and fresh definition. We hope you are encouraged and don't feel like we are banging you over your dome with the Bible.

In the spirit of MJ and Mamba, we don't want to just hear what is true, but do what is true. They were men of decisive action. So as you cross the bridge with us to connect faith and sports, seek understanding. Knowledge is everywhere today but people are not necessarily wiser. Understanding is far greater than knowledge. Right from the jump, we want to be clear that our intent is to grow your **faith**. How does faith happen? By hearing God's Word and acting on it so that you experience the amazing God of the Bible in your own life. To help make that happen for you, we share a promise from God at the end of each chapter. Since the beginning of time, God has never lied once and we are certain He will not start any time soon, especially with you. We trust that as you apply these seven words of life to your personal context, you will experience God's love as never before. We try not to be **hypocrites**, so know we are doing our best to live out these same seven promises from God.

In order to keep the rhythm of the read going, we have decided to list those who have gone before us in the 'Acknowledgements' section in the back. We certainly do not want to diminish the dedication of the many gifted, and tireless, journalists and authors. When you read an interesting insight, please give us no credit in your heart and mind, but know the hard work was done by the authors who have written on Jordan and Bryant.

We acknowledge the authors in the back rather than footnote every reference because we don't want your reading experience to feel like one of those NBA games where the referee calls way too many fouls. Isaac used to love to ride NBA ref Joey Crawford from his Laker Band perch. When Joey would make a senseless call, showboat with his silly 'that was a block' dance, and make it all about him, Isaac would yell at the court, "Joey, your face is not on the ticket. No one came here to see you!" Jesus, Jordan and Bryant's faces are on this ticket. So please be sure to check out our author acknowledgments at the end.

HOLY FIRE

As we prepare to experience *Jesus, Michael & Mamba*, we want to share an image that has guided God's people since the beginning: fire. Fire has always been synonymous with God's presence and leadership. He revealed himself to Moses as a flame of fire (Exodus 3:2). He lead Israel in the desert as a cloud of fire in the night (Exodus 40:38). When Elijah took on the 450 false prophets of Ba'al, he called on God to send holy fire from heaven (1 Kings 18:38). When the church began, all 120 faithful disciples received a personal tongue of fire (Acts 2:3). If you are reading this book, we believe that God is revealing His presence and beginning to light the fire of faith in your soul.

A few short months ago, my wife Becky and I (JT) experienced the holy fire of God in West Long Beach. She began to pray against two very shady businesses next to 5000 Pies, our award-winning social enterprise restaurant. The first business was a barber shop. When the new owners set up shop, they blacked out their glass windows and set up mattresses to sleep in the shop. Once their business opened, 5000 Pies would smell weed wafting through the vents and into our shop every day. And as one 5000 Pies high school interns astutely observed, "Yo, I ain't never seen anyone come out of there with a haircut." We were dealing with the 'Breaking Bad Barber Shop.'

The second business was a vitamin and herb business that did not sell vitamins or herbs. Instead this was a place where our neighbors went to worship idols, ask psychics to predict their future, and ask demons to bless their lives during the Covid-19 pandemic. Becky's heart mourned every time she saw a line out the door of people waiting to put their hope (and money) in dark idols. We were dealing with the 'Lucifer Vitamin Shop.' So Becky and our church family began to pray.

A few weeks after Becky began to pray, we received a call that a fire had broken out next to 5000 Pies. As we drove up to our restaurant, we saw the fire trucks and our hearts sank. We feared for our interns, employees and wondered what this meant for our work. When we arrived the Long Beach Fire Department captain said the barbershop was completed burned out. A garbage can full of chemicals exploded. 5000 Pies was the only store open and if we did not immediately call, the entire block would have gone up in flames. The barber shop was completely burned out and the street chemists fled. To this day, the barbers never returned to their shop.

Twelve days after the barber shop fire, the herb and vitamin shop also went up in flames. The same LBFD captain showed up again. At the botanica, he said the forensics revealed that a space heater overheated, launching a spark that landed directly on the **demonic** altar. All of the idols and demonic statues went up in flames. When our friend went to help the owners, he said he saw them weeping and screaming out, "Mi dinero, mi dinero!" The owners had placed all of the cash profits from the dark magic under the not so protective care of these false idols. The cash they hid under the altar went up in flames in a moment.

In 34 years the property owner said there had never been a fire. But once Becky began praying, the Lord gave the word from heaven, bringing two fires in twelve days. God's love for us is so great He will send His holy fire to burn away the dark things that destroy our lives. Will you take a moment to consider our first faith challenge? Whether you have been following Jesus all your life, or if this is your first time praying to God, will you join us in praying this short prayer?

"Father in heaven, as I read this book, please open up my heart and mind.

I want to experience your presence, your hope, and your love in my life. **In Jesus name, amen.**"

ON YOUR FEET

For over 40 years, as part of the Laker's pregame introductions at the Staples Lakers, Lawrence Tanter, the public address announcer would begin with the following opening invitation, "On your feet. It's time to greet the home team." The Lakers would emerge from the tunnel and take the court. With great anticipation, we offer you the same invitation.

"On your feet. It's time to greet Jesus, Michael and Mamba!"

Two cities.

Two teams.

Two pastors.

Two megastars.

One God who became flesh.

What time is it?

Game time!

FOUNDATIONS

And you know me
Turn a O-2 into the O-3, dog
Without 40, Oli', there'd be no me
'Magine if I never met the broskies
God's plan, God's plan

'GOD'S PLAN'
DRAKE

STAPLES CENTER AND GOD CREATING THE EARTH

Twenty minutes before the Lakers take the floor, Lawrence Tanter, the public address announcer of the Los Angeles Lakers begins every home game with the following words, "Welcome to Staples Center, the sports and entertainment center of the world." In 1998, this crazy sports and concert crib was just a concept. But a small nation of builders worked together and constructed 'The House that Kobe Built.' The statistics on this building are wild: 2,500 tons of structural steel; 19 millions pounds of rebar; 73,000 cubic yards of concrete; 14 miles of data cable; 2.8 million square feet of drywall; and 81,000 square feet of Terrazo tile. Put all of this together and you have a world-class basketball arena and concert hall that stands 150 feet high above the basketball court.

But to go high, you first must go deep.

I (JT) learned an important lesson as I rode my bike next to the hole that would become Kobe Bryant's new home court: To go up 150 feet you must first go down 2,630 feet.

We all have to start somewhere. Everyone of us, including Michael and Kobe, began at the exact same spot: the beginning. This word is the opening concept of **Genesis**, the first book of the Bible. 'In the beginning, God created the heavens and the earth' (Genesis 1:1). Did you know that just as the city planners, architects, general contractors, site foremen and construction workers had a plan to build Staples Center, so God also had a plan to create the world? But instead of thousands of skilled workers, God built the heavens and the earth with only His voice.

The first chapter of the Bible reveals God's blueprint for the world. Many of us are familiar with God creating the world in seven days. But did you know there is an order and structure to his design? The first three days were all about establishing the structural foundations: (1) Light so that the world would not be in **darkness**; (2) A clear spacer to separate the waters, creating the sky and the oceans; (3) Vegetation, fruit and seeds of it's own kind to bring forth food from the land. In three days, God had created the structural spaces and foods for humans to thrive on this planet.

The second three days were all about filling the amazing creation: (4) To provide light within this new globe, God filled the earth with light during the day (sun) and the greatest nightlight of all time (moon); (5) God filled the skies with birds, and the seas with fish and every sea creature; (6) And finally, God filled the land with **animals** of every kind and then brought forth His masterpiece, human beings (beginning with Adam and Eve) carefully creating each of us in His own image with His own hand. Humans are the only ones created in the image of God, spiritual beings with the capacity to think, make decisions and worship God. The Lord's plan for creating the earth is brilliant, methodical, detailed, and shows His amazing love for you and me. It is mind boggling that God created our world in six days with only His voice! Think about that the next time you walk outside, look into sky, and realize how big this world truly is.

At the beginning, everything in our lives happens to us or for us. None of us decided it was time to be born. No one determined what historical era we would live on planet earth. Why are you reading this book today? Why were you not born one hundred years ago in a different part of the world? No one picked their family (though some of us sure wish we could have had a do-over). No one picked our race, gender, personality, motivations, gifts, skills, or even our looks. The foundations period of our development is determined by the mind of God. He has the first word in our lives.

Let's zoom in and move from the cosmic realities to our here and now. It is amazing to consider God's methodical plans for families and individual people. He uses the same careful design that created the world in our own lives. As we consider our personal beginnings, we call this first stage of our lives 'Foundations.' While each of our stories and stages are different, we all share at least three common factors: family dynamics, character development, and critical incidents that shape us. As we first explore the foundation stages of our basketball mega-stars, we will also humbly offer reflections on our own foundations, before we ask you to reflect on your own foundations.

MICHAEL JORDAN FOUNDATIONS

The Jordans of Wilmington, North Carolina, were a successful upper middle class suburban Black family. In his book *Playing for Keeps*, historian David Halberstam introduces us to the the family that Michael Jordan grew up in. James Jordan was a military man, serving faithfully in the United States Air Force. After leaving the service, he became a mechanic at the General Electric Company. Everyone always talked about how gifted he was with his hands. Mr. Jordan could literally fix anything. You know he passed those great hands down to his middle son, Michael. James was a standout employee and became the general manager over three factory departments. The beautiful Mrs. Jordan had a rich personality, and was a much loved teller at their local bank. The Jordan family enjoyed three income streams: Mr. Jordan's GE check, an Air Force pension for his decorated service, and

Mrs. Jordan's salary. This gave the Jordan family the financial foundation they needed to provide significant opportunities for their children. Michael Wilbon's observation certainly rings true, "The Jordans were upper middle class. But there is a tendency in the media to move Black families down a notch in terms of class." So many stories around Black athletes exaggerate poverty, as if it were a badge of honor. As pastors of a churches that deal with poverty on a daily basis, there is nothing glamorous about poverty. No one gets street cred points for not having food on the table. As Tupac penned, "Life in the 'hood, it's all good for nobody." It's noteworthy that this was not the case with the Jordans or the Bryants.

Deloris Jordan had great expectations for her children. She drilled into her children to always work hard and never waste your talent. Of the five Jordan children, Michael confessed that he was always the laziest and got into the most trouble. Obviously, he grew out of that weakminded state and deleted the bad habits. His mother did not come down hard on him, but his mother was creative in her parenting and made sure he learned the life lessons he needed to succeed.

As a military man, James Jordan was all about discipline. He taught his children sports. Baseball, not hoops, was Mr. Jordan's passion. This helps us understand some of the emotions going on in Jordan's head when he shocked the world and retired from the NBA after collecting three straight chips. Michael did it for the memory of his dad. He did not leave the NBA because David Stern kicked him out for gambling. Jordan retiring literally cost the NBA millions of dollars in lost corporate sponsorship and future earnings. The NBA is a bidness and Stern was not about to kick out his golden cash cow. That theory is soft. (Think of when Kobe yelled at Dwight Howard...soft!)

Michael loved his father. He would be at his side both when he would work on his mechanical problems and play baseball. When focusing, Mr. Jordan would always stick his tongue out. It's a fresh reminder that for children, so much is caught and not only taught. Years later, Michael Jordan posters would hang on bedroom walls all over the world: Michael going to the rack with his tongue sticking out. Everyone wanted to 'Be Like Mike.' I wonder if they knew they were really trying to be like Mike's dad.

The key to Michael Jordan's ferocious competitiveness was Larry, his oldest brother. He was incredibly gifted as an athlete, but was only 5 feet 7 inches. We got nothing but love for Larry since we aren't the tallest pastors in America. If Larry had the height of his little brother, maybe Gatorade's jingle would have been 'Scary Like Larry.' Michael himself once said, "When you see me play, you see Larry play." The Jordan family was strong. James, Deloris and his siblings poured into Michael since his youth, cementing the values of hard work, maximizing God given talent, discipline, a love for sports, and even the hanging tongue.

Michael Jordan was able to soar to great heights because his family took him to great depths.

KOBE BRYANT FOUNDATIONS

Joe 'Jelly Bean' Bryant was from the Philadelphia area and fell in love with Pam Cox at La Salle University. Pam actually knew Joe as a child. Their grandparents lived very close to each other and were close friends. Romantic feelings for Joe surfaced the night Joe played her brother's college basketball team. Villanova played La Salle and after the game the Bryant and Cox families met on the court. Romantic fireworks began exploding at half-court. Jelly Bean was a big time athlete, but he also had some rough edges he was still working out. Pam was legit, organized, and locked in on becoming a lawyer. Some thought she would polish him up. Others thought he would bring her down. A Philadelphia reporter once quipped that Pam could have been the next big time lawyer but she chose to marry 'Crazy Joe Bryant.' Even against her father's wishes, Pam drew her line and married Joe. Ironically, the intensity (and speed) of their courtship would be mirrored years later by Kobe in his marriage to Vanessa Cornejo Laine. As luck would have it, the hometown Philadelphia 76ers drafted Joe. The Bryants were local heroes and everyone in the neighborhood was thrilled to see their friend make it to the NBA. Joe and Pam were off to a great start.

Kobe Bean Bryant was born on August 23, 1978. He was named Kobe because Pam was all about a local Japanese steakhouse during her pregnancy. Kobe steak is from Wagyu beef and is one of the most flavorful meats in the culinary world. This kind of beef is exported from Kobe, Japan. We have a church plant that we work with in Tokyo, and my friends Grant and Miho taught me the beef is pronounced 'ko-bay' (kō-bā), not the 'Kobe' chants that filled arenas for twenty years.

The naming of Kobe would prove to be a big theme for his foundation stage of life. Many fine dining experts believe Kobe beef to be the finest in the world because it is nurtured through a meticulous process. In the same way, Pam nurtured her son to become the finest in the world. Pam Bryant was a perfectionist and she passed on this trait to her son. Some authors note that Kobe and Pam enjoyed the closest bond possible between mother and son, digging a deep foundation for her son's ultimate achievement. As a professional athlete, Joe Bryant's life was full of airplanes, hotels and suitcases. He spent at least four months of every year on the road and his life was full of crazy demands even when home. But his career opened the door for Kobe Bryant to literally grow up inside the game of basketball.

Joe Bryant was not a star. While he had a magnetic personality like Kobe, he did not have the same talent or drive. He was a successful role player for the Philadelphia 76ers. Everyone who watched him ball would always talk about his sweet stroke. Like Vinny Johnson after him and Lou Williams in today's modern game, he provided instant offense from the bench. Everyone knew Mamba's dad as an explosive scorer with a beautiful jump shot. When the 76ers played home games, Kobe was with his dad every single game. Pat Williams was the General Manager of the 76ers during Joe's career and remarked that Kobe Bryant grew up in The Spectrum (the Philadelphia 76ers home crib from back in the day). Joe taught Kobe the game that would become his future. But Pam should be credited for instilling inside of him the resolute will and steely determination that would become known around the globe as 'Mamba Mentality.'

As Joe aged, his game slowed down and his NBA career ended in a minute. When that door closes, it closes fast and hard. The NBA is a business, and if you are no longer an asset, you are discarded. Joe still loved to ball and the family decided to play overseas. He received a contract offer to play ball in Rieti, Italy. This city north of Rome was so different from Philly, but it became the international basketball academy for young Kobe. He traveled with his dad to every practice, every home game, and almost every away game. Pro teams in Europe, unlike our teams in America, create youth versions of their team in their city. Kobe quickly became the star on Rieti's youth team. Kobe said "I learned fundamentals first in Italy. Most kids in America only focus on fancy dribbling. In Italy, they teach you true fundamentals and leave out all the nonsense."

In Italy, Kobe's father played with Mike D'Antoni. The gun slinger from West Virginia was the star of the team. This high-powered shooting guard became larger than life in Kobe's eyes. When signing to play with the Lakers, Kobe chose number 8 because D'Antoni wore number 8. Living in Italy helped Bryant appreciate global cultures, which would be critical in his friendship and on court chemistry with 'The Spainard' Pau Gasol. Bryant and Gasol won two titles for the Lakers speaking Italian and Spanish on the court. Together they contextualized many European values into the heart of the 2008-2011 Lakers.

After Joe Bryant's playing days were finished, the Bryant family moved back to Philly. This loving family that was already centered around basketball, re-emerged onto the youth basketball scene, as Kobe, their gifted, cultured, and focused young hooper exploded into the national limelight. The AAU basketball world quickly learned Kobe Bryant's name (though they would pronounce it wrong). And just like the Jordans, Joe and Pam Bryant methodically laid an incredibly strong runway of love, relationships, sports and laser focus from which Kobe would take off. It would be up to Kobe to determine how high he would go.

As we move from two global basketball icons to two very ordinary pastors, it is important for us to share a word of perspective. Jordan and Bryant were blessed by God with two amazing families. Not only did they have two sets of parents, but these parents were all-stars in their own way. In particular, the positive influence of Deloris Jordan and Pamela Bryant simply cannot be overstated. For many of us, however, what we experienced in our foundation years was not ideal.

Both of our foundations had serious cracks, which brought about so much pain and uncertainty, and have given both of us challenges to work through for our whole lives. And yet we have hope in God, the One who made heaven and earth, and has helped us work through really hard stuff. Here is a window into our stories.

MICHAEL THOMAS FOUNDATIONS

I (PMT) was born on March 21, 1977 at Michael Reese Hospital to Michael Sr. and Francine Thomas. Both my parents were born and raised in Chicago. My parents met in high school. My dad served in the military and is a Vietnam veteran who was one of countless soldiers who developed PTSD and drug addiction. In their first few years of marriage, we lived in California. By the time I was 3, my parents divorced and my mom and I moved back to Chicago. My father and I had an estranged relationship until I was 11, after that, it would be 20 years before I would hear from my father again.

My mom was an avid learner who had aspirations of becoming a lawyer. As a single parent, she worked full time and made a good life for us. To this day, I am so grateful for the sacrifice she made for her family.

My mom remarried and I gained a stepfather, and shortly thereafter, a baby sister. After several years, my family drifted away from church and things became rough within our family dynamic. As a teenager, my relationship with my stepfather was as bad as it could get. My mom and stepfather struggled in their relationship and there was constant tension and fighting (both verbal and physical) in our home. They ultimately divorced. At my lowest point, 16 years old, I ran away from home and even contemplated suicide.

Things were not looking good. My family looked nothing like MJ's or Kobe's. (But I'm not hating…well…maybe just a little.)

My mom is one of the strongest people I know. Our family was not perfect. But it was strong!

My spiritual life took off from a single invitation. Moms still had some loose ties to her faith community and one of her closest friends, Jamile Barnes, invited me to a youth event at her church. It changed my life forever. After a few months, I wanted to commit my life to Jesus. I even got baptized. I invited my family to the baptism ceremony and at that service, my family joined the church. This became a point of healing for our family and it made all the difference having Jesus in the true center of our lives. Jamile Barnes became a spiritual auntie to me!

While I was in graduate school, I was able to go through therapy since a part of my matriculation included serving as a crisis chaplain. And Christian therapy allowed me to process so much of the pain and brokenness I experienced in my childhood. No matter the family dynamic, we all have levels of brokenness, pain, joys, and strength within our families. And with the power of perspective, all experiences can serve as a classroom for us to grow from.

I love that Jesus invites us, not into religion or membership, but to be a part of His family. I also love the fact that Jesus' definition of family is not limited by homogeny, ethnicity, or class. I believe that in Jesus there is no dysfunction. In his family is unconditional love, affirmation, support, and guidance into being all we were created to be and like MJ and Mamba, encouraged to reach our full potential.

JOHN TETER FOUNDATIONS

I (JT) was born November 17, 1970 to Paul and Yung Soon Teter. My father was a Dutch man who grew up in Mobile, Alabama. My mother was born in what is today North Korea before Korea was divided into two countries at the end of World War II. My parents met on a steam ship that crossed the Pacific Ocean from Seattle to Seoul. My father worked on the ship as a mariner. But their 27 year marriage would end one day without warning.

My father was a glider plane pilot. The plane would get towed up to 10,000 feet and then my Dad would find wind channels and soar through the air like a bird. But one day his plane crashed. Our family would never be the same. I was ten years old.

While the plane crash changed my life forever, bad decisions almost derailed it. In eighth grade I began to medicate my pain. I was drawn to the cool kids who also came from broken families. We began to experiment with alcohol and drug abuse and were racing at high speeds towards a terrible crash.

One Saturday, after a night of partying and clubbing, my friends dropped me off at 1AM. It's not like I heard a voice, but I know something (or Someone) was telling me it was time to go home. Thirty minutes later, the friends I was with went and nabbed one of their father's guns to rob a drug dealer they knew.En route to the drug dealer's crib, they almost got into an accident on the freeway. My friend began arguing with the other driver. He then fired six rounds into the cab of the truck. The driver was hit three times. He was an off-duty police officer. The next day my friend's police sketch was the first story on the local Los Angeles news. My boy was sentenced to nine years in prison. My two other friends were sentenced to seven years for being in a car involved in a drive-by shooting. But the chair I was sitting in was empty. It was still warm, but empty. I missed seven years in prison by thirty minutes.

Years later, after I became a follower of Jesus, I thanked my Mom for not giving up on me. Even though we were not religious in any way (I can remember going to church only once as a kid), she told me about when she prayed for me. She said that one afternoon after a particularly horrible fight with me, she drove to the local Christian church. She entered the empty sanctuary with a blanket. She knelt before the cross and prayed a simple prayer, "Jesus, I do not know if you are real, but if you are, will you please take care of my son, John? I cannot do it anymore." She then symbolically wrapped me up as a baby in the blanket and left me at the foot of the cross.

Being rescued is the single dominant theme of my life. God has rescued me over and over again. My foundation stage was full of pain, loss and avoiding absolute disaster by 30 minutes. I attribute my faith today to the prayers of my wonderful mother. The Living God answered my desperate mother's prayers and He has taken such good care of me.

BASEMENT OR BALCONY

Whether our foundations are the penthouse of being born into an NBA family, or the basement of broken father dynamics, God's love for us is real. If you can look back on your foundations and rejoice at the structure God has built and the way He has filled it, we celebrate with you. Others of us, however, probably most of us, look back and have scars, wounds, and deep pain. We see response patterns in our lives that we wish never existed. We are constantly managing soul wounds that never seem to heal. If you look back on your foundations and feel sadness, shame, and pain, we hurt with you.

One critical element of faith is remembering that no matter where you come from, what matters is where you **finish**. There is always hope because we are given another day. Sometimes the blessings of God are so easy to see. But many of his most profound blessings take time, prayer, and a loving community around you to understand. In each of our foundations there are many clues about the future God has for us. The One who created the heavens and the earth has created you with a purpose in mind. A purpose that you must walk in faith to achieve. And when you explore the depths of your foundations, you will see the fingerprints of Almighty God who has loved you from before the beginning.

To reach great heights, you must first travel to the great depths.

SOUL DYNAMICS

- **BIBLE**

  In the beginning, God created the heavens and the earth. (Genesis 1:1)

- **REFLECTION**

  What critical incidents have shaped your foundation development stage?

- **PRAYER**

  Jesus, will You help me better understand the foundation you have created for me?

2

DESTINY

I'mma make it by any means
I got a pocket full of dreams
Baby, I'm from New York!
Concrete jungle where dreams are made of
There's nothing you can't do
Now you're in New York!
These streets will make you feel brand new
Big lights will inspire you
Hear it for New York, New York, New York!

'EMPIRE STATE OF MIND'
ALICIA KEYS

THE DRAFT LOTTERY SAVED MY LIFE

I (JT) met Alonzo at a backpack drive that our church was hosting for children in our underresourced neighborhood. Alonzo owns and operates Styles, Inc. a barber shop in West Long Beach. One end of summer afternoon we became friends at the Springdale Community Center. To bless the children before school starts, he transported his chair, brought his clippers, and gave free haircuts all day long.

A few years back I need a cut so I texted if his chair was open. He hit me with the thumbs up emoji for 5PM. Just as I was ready to roll out (4:55), Isaac texted me and asked if I was checking out the NBA draft lottery. I couldn't believe I almost forgot to watch one of my favorite events of the year. The Lakers had a 12% chance to move up in the draft. I texted Alonzo and told him I would head out after the draft lottery.

At 5:30 I pulled up to Styles, Inc. The po-po were everywhere. Yellow tape was across the front of the shop. A group of officers tried to hold me behind the line but I told them that I was Alonzo's pastor and needed to see him. They let me behind the line. I walked into the shop and I saw Alonzo being interviewed by a detective, as the forensics officer pulled glass shards off his shirt and body. They were taking pictures of all the glass on his body and in his hair for evidence.

I found out that Alonzo was talking next to his car with one of the homies in the neighborhood. Earlier in the week, this dude jacked a rival gang member's home for money, jewelry, drugs and his 90 inch tv. He talked too much and word got out he did it. As Alonzo was giving him counsel, the rival bangers saw him. They flipped a u-turn, crept real slow and opened fire on the barber shop. They were bad shooters. They missed their target but sprayed Alonzo's car and barber shop as everyone ran for cover.

I told Alonzo not to cut me. But he sat me down in the chair and said cutting would help him relax. We went back and forth between the drive-by and the NBA draft lottery. He said, "Pastor John, if you would have kept your original time, you might have got hit. Bullets started flying right around 5." As I sat in the chair, I thanked God for yet another example of God rescuing me.

The Lakers had a 12% chance for a higher pick hit. The Lakers moved up to number four in the NBA draft. The pick which had little value thirty minutes earlier had now become a valuable trade asset. This was a big part of the deal to bring Anthony Davis to La-La Land. As I left, Alonzo laughed, "Pastor John, the Lakers had a great night but you had a good night, too. NBA lotto might have saved your life!"

I believe that God worked through the NBA draft lottery to keep me out of the line of fire. Some might call this a coincidence. But PMT and I call it destiny!

WHAT IS DESTINY?

When someone thinks about the concepts of destiny they usually go to film. When Disney+ recently released the entire 'Star Wars' film series, a whole new generation was introduced to the epic battle of good and evil in the galaxy. I remember how I felt in the movie theatre as a little boy watching the Millennium Falcon soar through space. I see that same look in my children's eyes when they see the Mandalorian's Razor Crest light speed to the next adventure. And who could forget Luke and Darth and their light saber battle over the destiny of Luke Skywalker? Darth Vader proclaimed to his son (not a spoiler alert after 40 years) "Your destiny lies with me, Skywalker! Obi-Wan knew this to be true. Join me and we will rule the galaxy."

Here is how we define destiny: A meaningful event, person, or circumstance that helps us understand God's future plan for us. We believe in the depths of our souls that we do not create destiny, it has already been established for us. Just as the earth was already created for Adam and Eve, so our personal destiny has already been created by the One who created the heavens and the earth. In His great love for us, God becomes our friend, and in that growing love relationship, He begins to reveal our destiny. But it only becomes reality when we learn His ways and obey Him in the only path that leads to life.

DESTINY AND MICHAEL JORDAN

Four massive events aligned in one year, laying the foundation for Michael Jordan to become a true global icon. Dean Smith, Jordan's basketball coach at the University of North Carolina, prepared him to become the most dominant NBA player of all time. The Hall of Fame basketball coach was the first developmental piece in making Jordan the basketball player and towering global figure he would become.

David Stern was the second person who helped launch Michael Jordan to accomplish more than anyone could have ever imagined. In 1984, Stern became the commissioner of the NBA. He was a fast moving, silver-tongued New York City lawyer who specialized in marketing issues. He had a vision for what the NBA could become if they could market their stars, and not just teams, to the country.

When he took leadership over the NBA in 1984, all sports marketing was only based on teams. Stern gambled that marketing individual players, just like the tennis players who were getting all of the big endorsements, would grow the league. He began as the commissioner of the NBA looking for the perfect player to test his theory.

In 1984, cable television launched into American homes. Cable companies began beaming content into our living rooms. This would forever change how we consumed entertainment content, especially sports. Did you know that ESPN is an acronym? ESPN stands for Entertainment Sports Programing Network. Today, ESPN is like a family member for some people (babies have even been named ESPN and for the record, as pastors, we officially discourage that).The company took flight in 1984, the same year Michael Jordan exploded into the NBA atmosphere and the same year a marketing genius took over the NBA. But there was one more piece missing: products.

The final factor was a start-up shoe company in Portland, Oregon named Nike. Converse could not deliver on a shoe for MJ before his rookie season. Michael Jordan wanted to sign with Adidas but they straight up turned him down. This would turn out to be a multi-billion dollar mistake. Nike went all Public Enemy 'simple and plain, give me the lane' and offered Jordan a contract of $1 million for five years. At that time, that kind of money to endorse a shoe was unheard of. Little did Nike know they were signing the deal of a lifetime. In the first year, they projected the Air Jordan 1 (classic red and black color way) to profit $300,000. But in a matter of months, the Air Jordan 1 became a global phenomenon topping $133 million in sales. In a few years, Air Jordans became a fabric of our global society. Rappers rapped about the Jordans. Reporters reported on the Jordans. And children in Asia and Africa rocked the black and red kicks with pride.

Michael Jordan went on to fulfill his destiny as the first African-American global sports icon.

DESTINY AND KOBE BRYANT

As we analyze destiny patterns in Kobe's development, two meaningful circumstances stand out. In contrast to Jordan who saw four external factors align in a relatively short amount of time, Kobe's destiny incidents were internal and played out over close to a decade. Kobe Bryant knew from a young age that he would be a great NBA basketball player. Kobe was straight up bold in his prophecy that he would not only make it to the NBA, but that he would become one of the all-time greats.

As a kid who literally grew up in professional basketball arenas, Kobe not only had a passion for the game, but had what many would later call the 'it factor.' There was a showmanship to Kobe and his actions. People were drawn to him, even at a very young age. He was aware of that and would elevate his game for the crowds. When Joe Bryant played for the Italian city Tuscany, Kobe was one of the children who ran onto the court with a sweeper to mop up the sweat from the floor. The crowd at the 'Palace of Florence' loved Kobe and the way he would mop up the players sweat. Believe it or not, that became a thing. He would run out on the court to clean, sometimes when it wasn't needed. And people would roar with approval. From his earliest years, Kobe felt very comfortable stirring crowds to take notice and chant his name.

When he returned to the United States from living in Italy, his dream of NBA superstardom only grew stronger by the day. He mastered all of Magic Johnson's NBA title tapes. He ate, drank, and breathed basketball! In 6th grade, his teacher gave him an essay assignment, asking each student to present on what they wanted to be when they grew up. Kobe wrote with great detail that he would play in the NBA, and that he would be immortalized in the NBA Hall of Fame. After his presentation his teacher offered him some perspective and career counseling, suggesting before the class that he take a path that was the more stable and certain, "The odds of you fulfilling your plan are one in a million." Kobe defiantly fired back at his teacher, standing up before the whole class to declare, "I will be that one."

During his teen years, Kobe told everyone who would listen that he would become the greatest player in the history of the NBA. He did not lack for confidence. With every high school game, with every AAU tournament, with every tournament MVP honor, his declarations of future greatness came a little bit clearer into focus. There were still many haters, turned off by his shocking boldness. These predictions were met with head shaking and smirks. These kinds of dreams were ludicrous and impossible to fulfill. People thought Kobe Bryant was crazy.

By 1996, Kobe Bryant was a legend in Philadelphia and the national youth basketball network. Scouts, reporters and high school basketball fans flocked to Lower Merion High School to follow his every move. Most were blown away by his game, his charisma, and a confidence foreign to most every teen. In a spring press conference, the Lower Merion High School gym roared with approval when Kobe smirked, mugged and made the daring announcement, "I have decided to skip college and am taking my talents to the NBA!"

This was a daring move as he became only the sixth player in NBA history to skip college. But Bryant took the NBA by storm. And in 2010, LeBron James would pay homage to the Black Mamba when he told the world, "I am taking my talents to South Beach." Who can forget all of the midwesterners yelling at the bar television in rage and little kids burning their LeBron James jerseys in Cleveland? Meanwhile in Miami, all the Heat fans were hugging while ordering another mojito in South Beach.

Kobe Bryant went on to take his place as one of the greatest players to ever play the game.

THE WEEPING PROPHET

A pastoral note here is needed. For a very select few like Jordan and Bryant, destiny is lived out on a global stage by rising to the previously unknown heights in their chosen field. But Biblical destiny is lived out in our relationship with God. None of us will have Hall of Fame NBA careers. You might have followers on social media, but none of us will have millions upon millions of adoring fans. And we are not waiting on iconic shoe lines. However, each of us can be faithful to what God reveals in our own faith lives and communities. Destiny in the world is often defined by grand dreams and impressive achievements. Biblical destiny focuses on being faithful in a relationship with a loving God. This was true for one of the most celebrated **prophets** in the Bible, **Jeremiah.**

Most people think of a prophet as an angry man, usually with a personality disorder, holding up his Bible on a street corner, yelling at people as they walk by. But Jeremiah was a prophet called by God before He laid the foundations of the world (Jeremiah 1:5). God formed him and shaped him to be a person of truth, character, and most of all, love. So when Israel, the nation that he loved, fell into ruin because of sin, Jeremiah was not angry. He was sad. And because he shared his heart and allowed others to see his grief, he became known as the weeping prophet.

Jeremiah is famous for a few particular messages that filled his powerful sermons. Think of these sound bytes as pressers that go viral. He called Israel to remember the devotion of their youth and their loving commitment to God, "Israel, you have committed two evils: you have stopped drinking the living water; and you are drinking out of cisterns that hold no water" (Jeremiah 2:13). He lamented at how the moral fabric of Israel had unraveled, "They were not at all ashamed of their sin; nor did they know how to blush" (Jeremiah 6:15). Jeremiah went on to preach in a particularly depressing moment, after looking all around for healing from the wounds of sin, "Is there no balm in Gilead" (Jeremiah 8:22)? And with the skill of heart surgeon, he tried to help people understand that the problems in our world are not 'out there' but inside of our own heart. He preached, "The **heart** is **deceitful** above all things, and desperately wicked; who can know it" (Jeremiah 17:9)?

And yet, in the midst of such dark, troubled, and uncertain times, God spoke one of the greatest promises in the Bible through the weeping prophet. This was not just any promise, but an encouragement that dripped with destiny, overriding all of the circumstances Israel endured:

For I know the plans I have for you, declares the LORD, plans for welfare and not for evil, to give you a future and a hope. Then you will call upon me and come and pray to me, and I will hear you. You will seek me and find me, when you seek me with all your heart. (Jeremiah 29:11-13)

God promises that He has already established plans for His people. These plans are good. They are not evil. Think of God sitting on His throne and before Him is a cosmic white board with your life all planned out. Ten, twenty, thirty years are but a moment to God. And He oversees our lives, every intimate detail, to bring His plans to life. Do you know there is strategic plan from heaven and your name is on the binder? These plans provide you with not only a future, but a good future that is full of hope. God is not distant but He is very near. And He promises that when we seek Him with all of our hearts, we will find Him. Below are two illustrations of how we have called upon God, prayed to God, sought after God with all of our hearts, have experienced the Living God and have learned about his plans for our lives.

"JOHN, YOU WILL BE"

I (JT) decided to follow Jesus and commit to the narrow road of discipleship on May 8, 1992. And my destiny was revealed to me five days later. The weeks leading up to my decision of faith were filled with violence, injustice and the city of Los Angeles being set on fire. Rodney King, a young African American man, had been pulled from his car and mercilessly beaten by four white police officers. The police brutality case became a global story. Grainy video footage captured every gruesome detail. Who can forget the picture of King's beaten and swollen face? If you are younger and have not heard about Rodney King, please Google him and learn.

The trial was moved from Los Angeles County to the city of Simi Valley. The courts believed the arrested officers would get a more fair trial in an all white affluent community. The clear evidence was ignored by a racially prejudiced all-white jury. Every officer was acquitted of every charge. When word of this kangaroo court verdict was released, people in Los Angeles rose up in defiant despair.

Looting, flames, violence and loss lasted ten days. I believe God used this incident to reveal part of the work He had me to do. From that first day, I knew part of my calling would be to work towards uniting race and class in the Kingdom of God.

I became a disciple of Jesus apart from church. In my first year away at college I joined a dorm Bible study. After seven months studying the Bible I found what I had been looking for all of my life and surrendered to Jesus. I told some friends about it and they invited me to a bbq a local pastor was hosting for college students.

Other than my friend, I had never met any of the 30 people at the study. The pastor grilled some killer bbq and then invited us all into the living room. He said we would open up with singing. I had no idea there was Christian music. This might be new for some of you reading this book. I listened to these foreign songs, mouthed some words, and wondered if they were going to pull out lighters for the slow jams.

I did not know this, but Pastor Ken and his ministry team were very strong in the spiritual gift of **prophecy.** He would listen to God, hear his Voice, and then deliver a timely message that came directly from God. When the last song was over, I thought it was time for dessert. But Pastor Ken said, "Now it is time for prophecy." He lifted up his bowed head, looked me in the eye and said, "We will begin with John. Will you please stand up?"

Overwhelmed, confused, and weak in the legs, I somehow managed to stand. Pastor Ken looked me in the soul and began to speak the word of the Lord. The Lord God spoke a two-fold personal prophetic message to me through the pastor:

"John, your commitment to Me is real. I receive you as My son and your sins are forgiven. And you will be a teacher of My Word. Many will hear your teaching and respond to Me in faith."

When the pastor finished his prophecy, I heard some gasps from the students, a few people began clapping and I can't explain why, but I began to weep. A complete stranger who had no idea I made my decision to commit to God five days before, confirmed for me what was true in the spiritual word. And he clearly defined my destiny. Not only had God welcomed me into his family as his son, but he had a special role assignment for me. I was to become a teacher of the Bible. (Writing this book with Pastor Michael Thomas is one way I am fulfilling my destiny to be a teacher of the Word).

When the prayer meeting ended, a short man in a sweat stained shirt (it was blazing hot in that living room) approached me. He was kicking it in the back and putting in work. His role was to tape the prophecies and record them on a cassette tape. He handed me a cassette tape, with a Sharpie scribbled title: 'John, May 13 1992.' Today, the tape sits on my prayer desk reminding me of God's grace to me and my responsibility to fan into flame the gift God has given to me. On a funny note, when my children noticed the audio tape one day, they asked me, "Daddy, what is that?" I explained that it is an 'ancient iPod that recorded Daddy's destiny.' I am surprised the kids didn't start speaking to the cassette tape, calling her Siri or Alexa.

Christian destiny is not about achievement, but about relationship. And whenever I study and preach the Word of God I know I am doing what I was made for. And I learn more and more about God's plan to give me a good and happy future.

"MICHAEL, YOU WILL BE"

We all are inspired when we hear the destiny process that Michael and Kobe experienced. The great thing is that destiny and the process one goes through in reaching one's destiny is not exclusive to NBA Hall of Famers. I believe that we all have a destiny, a future that God has ordained for us that is full of goodness and hope.

What is amazing is that destiny doesn't just happen in a microwave, it happens in the oven! Can we be honest for a moment? Microwave meals are edible; but the food always tastes better in the oven. Can I get a witness from someone in the back? In the same way, destiny doesn't just happen in a 30 seconds moment, but it is an oven-roasted, slow cooking process that happens over time.

I (PMT) was born and raised in Chicago. Even after accepting Jesus in my life at 17 years old, I still thought I would study and go on to college to become an architect. The first clue of my destiny was how I came into my senior year of high school with a stronger desire to start a youth bible study club at my school than I did attending my CAD drawing classes.

By the time I was 20, going to college and working construction, I remember hearing God's voice. This was not an audible voice like someone yelling at me from down the block. But this was an inner voice that was speaking to my spirit. I heard the Living God say to me,

"Michael, I am not calling you to build buildings. You will be building people."

By age 24, I was convinced that God was calling me to pastor a local church. What I did not anticipate was God calling a kid from the south-side of Chicago — the 3rd most segregated city in America at the time, to start an intentionally multiethnic church in....Seattle!

This seemed so crazy to me because I had never experienced multiethnic anything at that point. And I certainly had no tangible connections to Seattle. As a matter of fact, the only things I knew about Seattle were the SuperSonics and how my Bulls put it on them in '96 (sorry, not sorry Seattle), the television show Frazier, a small little software company called Microsoft, and something called a Space Needle. You know this left me with a thousand questions and even more uncertainty. But I began experiencing a strange, almost supernatural peace. This often happens when we start slotting into the good and happy future God has for us. I became more and more aware, that no matter the cost, the safest place for me and my growing family to be was in the will of God. So after much prayer, my wife Kim and I yielded to God's will and allowed ourselves to accept this as a part of God's destiny for us.

There is something about recognizing destiny that fuels you to a new level of focus and sacrifice. I remember Kobe Bryant once sharing about the moment when he essentially accepted his destiny and made the conscious decision to focus and sacrifice for it. It was right after he and Brandi went to prom. He was a young rookie and talked about being at a stoplight driving his car. A group of kids his age were crossing the street. Kobe shared how this group was laughing, having fun, and just enjoying life. He shared how they would never know how much he envied them in that moment. But Kobe said that he instantly asked himself a question: "Do you want to have fun or do you want to be great?" The answer to his own question is what started him on his path to achieve his destiny. He went on to blow that up into what today we know as the 'Mamba Mentality.' I like to think that I too, once accepting the destiny that lay before me, developed my own sense of Mamba Mentality to see where this destiny in Seattle would lead.

My process started with me going back to school. I worked full time during the day, served as an associate minister in my church, and even with a wife and growing family, went to night school to complete my undergraduate degree in Church and Ministry Management. After graduating, destiny struck as I became the first recipient of a new scholarship that allowed me to go to seminary full-time. My wife and I made the difficult decision for me to quit working and pursue seminary full time. We moved next to the college campus, placing my family in the 2nd most diverse zip code in the country for 3 years. God was preparing us for Seattle.

God blessed us with a church denomination who didn't just talk about it, but actually started new churches with a heart towards diversity and reconciliation. We started Radiant Church in 2013, in Seattle, one of the most unchurched cultures in America. Today, God has blessed us to become a thriving, multi-ethnic church that has become a light for the city of Seattle. And while the church is amazing and one of the joys of our lives, it is my relationship with God that I most treasure. He has fulfilled the promise He made to me when I was 20 years old. He has given me hope, and a good, happy future. And honestly, it blows my mind that all of what I experienced was on God's white board decades ago. Who is like our God?

It is so hard to describe the feeling of fulfilling even part of your destiny. I guess it's like winning 6 championships? There is nothing like knowing you are exactly where you are supposed to be. To find your own destiny and be willing to go through the process of pursuing destiny, there is nothing that makes me feel more alive, not only in body and mind, but in spirit. There is no cookie-cutter destiny for us all to try and fit into. You don't have to be 23, 8, or 24. You just have to be the one who desires a deep connection with the coach of your life. Seek him with all of your heart and you will find Him. And He will show you your destiny. Then you have a choice: reject it and do what you think is safe, or accept it and take the greatest journey of your life. You will find yourself at the stoplight of your life, asking the same question as Kobe.

Choose wisely.

Choose God, and He will reveal to you your **eternal** destiny!

SOUL DYNAMICS

● **BIBLE**

For I know the plans I have for you, declares the LORD, plans for welfare and not for evil, to give you a future and a hope. (Jeremiah 29:11)

● **REFLECTION**

What critical incidents, special people and/or unique talents guide you as you journey into your destiny?

● **PRAYER**

Jesus, please encourage me into the future and hope you have prepared for me.

3

DRIVE

To protect my position, my corner, my lair
While we out here, say the hustlas prayer
If the game shakes me or breaks me
I hope it makes me a better man
Take a better stand
Put money in my moms hand
Get my daughter this college plan, so she don't need no man
Stay far from timid
Only make moves when your hearts in it
And live the phrase sky's the limit

'SKY'S THE LIMIT'
NOTORIOUS B.I.G.

MAMBA DAY, BIG GAME JAMES & THE SAT

April 13, 2016 is affectionately known around the basketball world as "Mamba Day." That Tuesday evening the Los Angeles Lakers hosted the Utah Jazz in the last game of the season. It was also the final game of Kobe Bryant's career. When Kobe announced in January that his twentieth season in the league would be his final campaign, ticket sales for the otherwise unremarkable April 13th game blew up on all of the secondary market sites. Everyone wanted to celebrate the career of Kobe and be in the building for the last time he laced up the Kobes XIs.

As a member of the Lakers Band, I make two or three videos a year capturing big events: the band performing the national anthem on the floor, special and big games, and even championship parades. I was excited to capture Kobe's last game on film. When I took the elevator down to the event level, I felt such a strong buzz from the crowd, but it was a very different pregame experience. During an intense playoff series the lower bowl of the Staples Center is full of nervous energy. Must win games come with knots in our stomach. Our crowd chants "Let's go, Lakers" over and over not only as a pledge of our undying allegiance, but also as a wishful hope almost willing the Lakers to execute on the court that night. But 'Mamba Day' was an altogether different animal.

'Mamba Day' was all about love. There were no expectations. There was no threat of elimination. There was no title to claim. It was the final 48 minutes in a four month farewell tour. It was a giant Black Mamba party. For the record, Michael Jordan scored 15 points in his final game. Shaquille O'Neal scored zero points in 4 minutes in his last game. But Kobe Bryant dropped 60 points in his last game, further cementing his legend as one of the greatest basketball players of all time.

Every major media site in America, and what seemed like all of Asia, flooded the Staples Center floor that night. I cruised by Hollywood A-listers like Jack Nicholson, Denzel Washington, and Leonardo DiCaprio. I walked by Flea from the Red Hot Chili Peppers warming up in the tunnel (Kobe requested he do a bluesy rendition of the national anthem on his guitar for his last game, but in a twist of fate he could not stay for the game since the band was performing at a concert on Sunset Blvd). Jay-Z, Beyonce, and Adam Levine were in the house. Kendrick Lamar asked me if he could scoot by so he could walk onto the court and give Kobe one last big hug.

For the video I grabbed unscheduled interviews with former players, celebrities and Lawrence Tanter, the Lakers public address announcer for forty years. I had a nice interview with Big Shot Rob (Robert Horry) and Big Game James (James Worthy) who were court side to cover the pre-game for Spectrum Sports Net. I shared with Worthy a somewhat shameful story, from my teen years.

"James, you have no idea how much I loved your 'Showtime Lakers' as a kid."

"I'm glad you liked the squad," he responded.

"Do you know that I chose watching your 1987-88 Game 7 title over going to a university?"

"What are you talking about, man?" he asked.

"I only took the SAT once," I said, "But my test day was June 20, 1988. That was your Game 7 against the Pistons. Tip-off was 12:30 and my friend was throwing a big party. I dropped my pencil mid-test and walked out because I was not missing Game 7!"

"C'mon, man, you didn't!"

"I got a 600 in English but a 180 in math because I bounced to watch you ball!"

James Worthy looked me in the eye and said, "Wow, man. You were crazy."

I wanted to say, "Hey I'm on the floor of Kobe Bryant's last game talking to you, so it all worked out." But instead I just gave him a fist bump and went to my next interview.

On the night when all of NBA royalty came out to honor Kobe Bryant's unmatched work ethic, I confessed to Big Game James that I walked out in the middle of my SAT. Looking back, I am honestly shocked at the lack of drive in my life. And I am glad Rick Singer wasn't a thing back in the day or I might have been in that Netflix documentary.

LET ME GUARD THEIR BEST

Inside all of us, there is a fire to create, to achieve, and to make a significant impact in our world. Very few of us have the discipline or the focus to fulfill our greatest dreams. Many of us make decisions while thinking that we are not making decisions. We default into lives of mediocrity. We settle. Then many years later we look back and wonder aloud what could have been. Our dreams will lead us down a road and when we see the challenge or obstacle we think to ourselves, "I just can't." Michael Jordan and Kobe Bryant found a way to overcome each and every obstacle. We believe one of the secrets to their formula for success was a drive that simply would not be denied. They never said "I can't" because they understood "Can't really means won't." They embraced pain, suffering, and countless costs to achieve their goals.

Michael Jordan and Kobe Bryant were two of the most driven (and talented) human beings that have ever walked the face of the earth. Their work ethic is legendary. Their drive for success is unparalleled. When the most talented player on a basketball team is also the hardest worker, success is inevitable. There is story after story about how 23 and 8/24, even after drinking from the chalice of success, would continue to run through the wall. Unlike most of us, this fire only burned fiercer when they reached the top.

In 2006, Kobe Bryant committed to the USA men's basketball team, two years after the team suffered a humiliating loss to Argentina in the 2004 Olympics. The 2008 team was called 'The Redeem Team.' Kobe Bryant focused his burning drive to bring America back the gold. Duke legend and then head coach of USA Basketball, Mike Krzyzewski tells the story of the first time the team gathered. Team USA met at the Wynn Hotel in Las Vegas. During the dinner Kobe asked Coach K if they could speak outside.

"Coach K, can you do me a favor?"

"And what's that?"

"I want you to let me guard the best player on every team we face," Kobe said.

"You are the greatest offensive player in the game," said Coach K. "Why are you asking me to play defense at the highest level?"

"Coach," answered Kobe, "I promise you that I will destroy him."

Kobe Bryant had scored 50 or more points ten times that past season. He dropped 81 points on Jalen Rose and the Raptors only seven months earlier. But his commitment was to destroy on defense. He was sending a message to Team USA. Kobe Bryant was willing to adapt to a different role to help the team reach their highest goals. His relentless drive for the gold medal manifested in defense.

HOW DO I IMPROVE MYSELF?

When Michael Jordan was a student at North Carolina, he told his roommate, Buzz Peterson, that someday there would be a sneaker line named after him. Peterson replied, "Michael, they haven't named a sneaker after Larry Bird or Magic Johnson and they are NBA stars." After Michael signed his first contract with Nike, he called his friend Buzz. He told him, "Buy stock in Nike because the 'Air Jordans' are going to take off!" Peterson thought his old college friend had a really big head.

But Michael Jordan was just listening to the inner fire that drove him to greatness. The context is remarkable. Jordan just completed the transition from college to the NBA. The number of games played in a season leapt from 30 to 82. Most first year players run into what is called 'the rookie wall.' Jordan ran right through that wall. He was named 1984-85 NBA Rookie of the Year. He averaged 28.2 points, 6.5 rebounds, 5.9 assists and 2.4 steals in 82 games. But he was not satisfied. He was not hungry, he was hawngry, for more! So he called his old assistant coach at University of North Carolina for honest input.

"Coach," Michael asked, "What do I need to do to work on my game?"

"Well Michael, you just won NBA rookie of the year. What more do you need?"

"No, I need you to be honest with me," Michael said, "What can I do to improve myself?"

"Michael, if you improve your jump shot, you will be unguardable. No one can ever sag off you and you can blow by them whenever you want," replied Coach Williams.

That summer, Michael Jordan shot jump shots in an empty gym until his arms fell off. Coach Roy was right. No one was able to guard Michael Jordan once he improved his jump shot. Jordan applied that powerful internal drive to his game and rode it hard all the way to 6 NBA titles, and even in pursuit of a career in major league baseball.

When we think of the legendary drive of Kobe and Michael, the old Gatorade ad pops into our mind. Back in the day Gatorade marketed their sugar water with the question, "Is it in you?" The company paid millions of dollars to make every one think that if they drank their drink then suddenly this drive would burn in our lives. If it could only be so easy! We openly confess that we do not know all of the factors that lead to drive. We might not know how it gets there, but we certainly know it when we see it. And when we scan the Old Testament there is one young man (and his three friends) who burned with fire for God.

DANIEL AND HIS THREE FRIENDS

One of the greatest disciples in the Bible is **Daniel**. He was not a **pastor**. He was not a traditional prophet, but he was a **lay leader** called and appointed by the Lord Jesus. He was not even from the **Levitical priest line**, which would have made him expected to do religious stuff. He was a regular guy who worked for the government. Against his will.

When Daniel was a young boy, King Nebuchadnezzar of Babylon took control of Jerusalem. The Babylonian army ransacked the city and as is the custom in ancient war, most of the best and brightest were taken from the conquered nation, to insure that they would not able to rebuild anytime soon. Imagine if this happened in the NBA. What if a team eliminates another team during a playoff series and they not only advanced but took that teams' next year's first round draft pick. That happened to Jerusalem. And Daniel was a first rounder.

When Daniel was 13 years old he was trafficked and forced into captivity. Leaving behind all he knew and loved, Daniel found himself in Babylon. There were likely thousands of young boys that were kidnapped, but the Biblical story highlights Daniel and his three Hebrews friends, Hananiah, Mishael, and Azariah. These four became a bonded band of brothers as they were indoctrinated in the wisdom, skills, and ways of Babylon.

But Daniel and his three friends had crazy drive inside. They resolved that they would not defile themselves with the King's food or the wine that he drank (Daniel 1:8). His inner resolve was so strong that he stood up to the greatest King in all of the world. He and his friends said they would not cross the line and worship foreign gods, no matter the cost. This drive for faith would deliver them from cultural pressure. They would go on to be thrown into a fiery furnace and yet the Lord delivered them without singeing a hair on their heads (Daniel 3:27). At 73 years old, Daniel was thrown into a den of ferocious lions, and he ended up taking a nap on the belly of a lion while the other hungry lions calmly watched him sleep (Daniel 6:22). Today, Daniel is the most outstanding example of a young disciple full of drive for Jesus, who was able to sustain that fire all the way to the end, even under unimaginable circumstances.

PREACHING, HOOPS & GIDEON THOMAS

I (PMT) love **preaching** the Word of God! I can't believe my job is to study, preach, and teach the Bible. Whether you have grown up in the church or are new to the faith, preaching is not easy.

Preaching, true and real preaching, is no doubt an enterprise we cannot do without the Holy Spirit. Preaching is also something that you will fail at if you only rest on your gifts or talent. It is something we must rely on the the Holy Spirit to do and then with great humility, work at developing your talent. Kevin Durant once said "Hard work beats talent every time talent fails to work hard." Like Durant, what Michael, Mamba and any basketball great share in common is that they all understood, talent is not enough. Talent must be matched with an equal or greater work ethic.

I began preaching 20 years ago. I was told early I had a gift or talent for it. In my early ministry years, I was fortunate to have a pastor and mentor who saw my gift and opened doors for my talent to be nurtured. My pastor at the time, Charles Jenkins, instilled in me the necessity to study, work, and prepare well when it came to opening the Word of God. I will never forget one of my early sermons at Fellowship Baptist Church. I was preaching on 2 Chronicles 7:14. My sermon was titled "What Do You Do When God Goes Deaf?" As a young preacher, the church had mercy on me and encouraged me throughout the delivery of the message. Pastor Jenkins shared with me after I finished, about the danger of my title and reminded me that nothing is wrong with God's hearing. The point he rightly made was do not be so focused on having a dramatic title, but to make sure your title makes sense. I thought I had blown my chance. I heard Eminem in my ear, "You only get one shot, don't miss your chance to blow." I thought I would never get another opportunity.

But right after he said that, he said, "So let's schedule your next sermon." From there he trained me, taught me **Bible study habits,** proper sermon preparation, and taught me how to design and organize a sermon. At the time, he was my MJ of preaching and what I saw was an amazing work ethic— paired with talent and the Holy Spirit. I was inspired and it instilled in me the belief that "hard work beats talent when talent fails to work hard."

In the same way that there are all kinds of basketball players who have diverse styles of play, there are also all kinds of preachers, styles, and gifts. The best do not rely on talent alone but they study, work, and prepare. In other words, they match talent with work ethic.

My youngest son's name is Gideon. He is tall and lanky. I am 5'9" and Gideon is only 14 and already as tall as me (thank God he got my good looks and not my height). He is an amazing basketball player with undeniable talent. But we noticed early on that he could improve in his work ethic. He began playing AAU ball and he soon learned for himself that kids with less talent but stronger work ethic ended up defeating him. I am excited to see the basketball player he will become as his work ethic matches and even surpasses his talent.

I want to encourage you to proactively develop an equal appreciation for work ethic as much as talent. If you are someone who is blessed enough to know your gift or talent, don't let it become lazy. Work hard as if you did not have talent. Work as if you had to compensate for a lack of talent. Work hard because with talent, working hard will ensure success. Hard work is one of the key components of Godly character. Working hard says something— not about what you can do, but it speaks to who you are! You are counted among those who do not settle low. You separate yourself from those who only reach for low hanging fruit. Hard work declares that you are one who will run through the wall, never cut corners and persevere when things get hard. Those who burn with fire become people of excellence.

We must remember that talent itself is not the destination, it's the vehicle to get to the destination. And work ethic is the fuel, it's the plug in (for all you electric and hybrid car lovers), that propels the vehicle to the destination. For me, preaching in and of itself is not the destination. The destination is to tell someone about Jesus and his love for all of us. Preaching is my vehicle to get to that destination and work ethic is what fuels my vehicle.

When you rest on talent alone, you face a deep temptation to start thinking it's all about you. And like a car without fuel, like a car without proper charging, no matter how beautiful the car, you will find yourself falling short of making it to your destination.

THE DREAM AND THE KILL

We end this chapter with an illustration from the 2008 USA Basketball Team and a quote from the Black Mamba that helps us understand his mentality and approach to life and basketball. The following quote is the core message of the 'Mamba Mentality' philosophy. Coach K kept one email from Kobe Bryant during the 2008 redeem team. Kobe wrote:

"I've been thinking a lot about our US team. I cannot wait to get started. I've been watching a great deal of European ball. Trying to learn their movements and tendencies. I am ready to learn and I am excited to be coached by you. You are one of the best. I look forward to the thrill of a new challenge and the joy of a new kill."

And finally, Kobe spoke these words from the Staples Center Lakers logo when he became the only player in the history of the NBA to have two numbers retired by the same team. Kobe shared the secret to work ethic and drive at his number retirement ceremony.

"Those times when you get up early and you work hard. Those times you stay up late and you work hard. Those times when you don't feel like working. You're too tired. You don't want to push yourself, but you do it anyway. That is actually the dream."

May you pray to God the Father, to Jesus the Son, and to the Holy Spirit, who makes it all happen in our lives, asking for the the fire. Just as He did for Daniel, He will set your soul on fire. And you will be different.

Is it in you?

SOUL DYNAMICS

● **BIBLE**

But Daniel resolved that he would not defile himself with the king's food, or with the wine that he drank. Therefore he asked the chief of the eunuchs to allow him not to defile himself. (Daniel 1:8)

● **REFLECTION**

In what areas of your life do you experience drive? In what areas of your life do you need more fire?

● **PRAYER**

Jesus, please grant me the same faith drive that you gave to Daniel.

TEACHERS

Somebody shoulda told me it would be like this
Be like this, be like this
Somebody shoulda told me it would be like this
Yeah, false prophets

'FALSE PROPHETS'
J. COLE

MRS. TETER'S OPUS

The odds were against my mother becoming a teacher in America. Yung Soon Whang grew up in Seoul, Korea and as a little seven year old girl she carried the dream of becoming a second grade teacher in America. How would a little girl make it across the world to fulfill her dream when there were massive obstacles, even in her own home? I never met my grandfather on my Mom's side. But Mom told me he was old school. It was Korea in the 1940s and he told her that her job was to cook, clean, and make babies. But he died early due to the war. My grandmother, who I did get to meet and spend many years with, was able to see the future and encouraged her daughter to pursue her dream. Mom crushed high school. She smashed the elite university in Seoul. And she found herself in New York City, leaving behind her mother and six brothers, to achieve a masters degree in teaching from Wagner College. She would proudly state that she was the only Asian

Drive

at the college, during the Korean War, and she loved it. My Mom had a legendary drive and modeled for me what it means to be a trail blazer and pioneer.

Yung Soon Teter taught second grade at Don Julian School in a small suburb of Los Angeles for 45 years. She loved teaching and the students loved learning from her. I count it one of my great blessings in life to spend every day with a teacher. She was always asking me questions, teaching me to learn for myself, and provided me with countless growth opportunities. My Mom will always be my first and most beloved teacher in all my life. Growing up, I just thought she was going to work. Occasionally, I would help her prepare her room at the end of summers. But I never really understood what she did. That changed on the day of her retirement.

Just as the Lakers and the NBA pulled out all of the stops for the 'Mamba Farewell Tour,' Don Julian Elementary made sure that Mom knew how much she was loved and appreciated as one of the greatest teachers in the land. I had the honor of sitting next to her at her retirement banquet. The principal, administrators and fellow teachers filled the auditorium with streamers and balloons. The principal honored my mother for her consistent excellence in teaching over four decades. The vice principal thanked my Mom for shattering stereotypes and building multi-ethnic community. Her peers affirmed my Mom's learning posture and how inspiring it was to have a Korean woman not only learn Spanish, but effectively teach as a bilingual teacher. And I will always treasure the memory of the four generation Latino family thanking my mom for being their favorite teacher. It was incredible to hear the bisabuelo (great grandfather), abuelita (grandmother), madre and padre (mother and father both had my mom as their second grade teacher), and niño, pour out their hearts about how much they loved Mrs. Teter!

Yung Soon Teter was a truly remarkable teacher and inspires me everyday to learn first and then teach.

DEAN SMITH & MICHAEL JORDAN

Jesus teaches that when a **disciple** is fully trained they will be like their teachers (Luke 6:40). This is true for disciples in the Kingdom of God, and also for basketball players. Dean Smith was the primary teacher of Michael Jordan who prepared him to become Air Jordan.

Coach Smith was born February 28, 1931. He was inducted into the basketball Hall of Fame after coaching for 36 years at the University of North Carolina, Chapel Hill. He recorded 879 victories, won 2 national titles, and coached the Tar Heels to 11 Final Fours. But so many of these accomplishments are overshadowed by the values he lived by and methodically taught his players.

Dean Smith's Tar Heel basketball program never had a scandal. He insisted his students earn their college degrees, boasting a 96.6% graduation rate. He was a champion of racial equality and promoted unity across races during the civil rights movement in the South. He recruited Charlie Scott, UNC's first African-American scholarship player. He challenged racist local business owners because of their unequal treatment of Black men and women. As the celebrated UNC coach, he used his authority to make life very difficult for owners who continued in their racist ways. As the Carolina 'Ball Coach' he operated as a champion for civil rights.

Dean Smith won his first national championship in 1982. This team featured three NBA players: 'Sleepy' Sam Perkins, 'Big Game' James Worthy, and an incredibly talented but raw freshman named Michael Jordan. Coach Smith ran a very structured program built on a tradition of upper class leadership, but Coach Smith personally invested in Jordan and came to trust him. This had never happened before in Coach Smith's program. He knew very early on that Jordan was special.

In the 1982 championship game, Jordan's Tar Heels battled Georgetown. The Hoyas had an incredible defensive unit anchored by Patrick Ewing. In the final seconds of the game, North Carolina was down by one point but had possession of the ball. They could win the game with a basket. Coach Smith called for the last shot to go to the freshman, Michael Jordan. In the huddle, Coach Smith looked Jordan in the eye and said, "Michael, knock it in!" Michael did exactly as his coach asked. The 1982 NCAA championship game winning shot was the first big notch in what would become the legend of Michael Jordan.

Coach Smith's leadership and mentoring extended well beyond the basketball court. Dean Smith taught his players integrity. He stressed that the values he taught them need to be integrated into their daily lives. To not live by your own code would make you a hypocrite. Jordan tells the story of a classmate urging him to park in a handicap spot. He even tempted him that no one would do anything to him since he won the school the national chip. But even though he was late for class, Jordan replied, "If Coach Smith ever knew I parked in a handicap zone he would make me feel terrible and I would never be able to face him." Michael Jordan had such a strong respect for his teacher, he chose integrity in his daily life, happily making the long walk from the outer parking lots to his class.

In Jordan's rookie year with the Chicago Bulls, he absolutely smashed the league in a way no other rookie had ever done before. He ran away with the Rookie of the Year trophy and even earned second team All-NBA honor. After one of his 40 point explosions, a reporter asked him, "Michael, is Dean Smith the only one in the world who could hold you to 15 points a game?" (In North Carolinas, structured offense Jordan averaged 17.7 points a game.) With steel in his eyes, Jordan looked the reporter in the eye and and said, "Coach Smith did not hold me to 15 points. Coach Smith taught me to score 40 in the NBA."

Dean Smith was a truly remarkable teacher. And when Jordan was fully trained, he became like his teacher.

PHIL JACKSON & KOBE BRYANT

Phil Jackson was the primary teacher of Kobe Bryant (and a great influence on Michael Jordan) and prepared him to become the Black Mamba. Phil Jackson was born September 17, 1945 in Deer Lodge, Montana. He was the son of a pastor and grew up in the church. Jackson always remembered how his father honorably removed a minister who had fallen into adultery. Jackson also writes that he never forgot the pain of ministry, as his father did his best to counsel a church member who caused a horrific car accident with his grain truck. The man eventually committed suicide and it was a young Phil Jackson who answered the call from the grieving wife. He was the one who would break the news to his father.

After a very successful college career, the broad-shouldered Jackson was drafted by the New York Knicks. He was never the star, but was a vital role player coming off the bench to provide aggressive defense and just enough timely scoring. Being on the bench to start the game gave Phil Jackson a perspective to appreciate all 12 members of a basketball team. There is a clear pattern. Many of the greatest coaches were role players in their playing days. This is often the secret sauce to becoming great team builders. The superstars often make terrible coaches because they cannot understand why others are not as gifted, as driven or as clutch as they were. Clearly defined roles for every member of the 12 man roster would become a defining characteristic of all Jackson coached teams.

After many years of bouncing around the hard and lonely roads of the minor leagues (including years of coaching overseas in hostile, and even dangerous, foreign gyms), Phil Jackson became the coach of the Chicago Bulls. Jackson was committed to a method of studying individual player personalities, meditation, yoga, and assigning books and book reports to each player. John Salley, a player on both the Bulls and Lakers said, "He was the greatest student of people I've ever been around. He knew exactly which buttons to push." Jackson ended up winning 11 NBA championships; six with Michael Jordan and the Bulls and five with Kobe Bryant and the Lakers. Phil Jackson would go on to become the basketball teacher that most impacted the life and career of Kobe Bryant.

Many have written that Kobe killed college basketball. Before the Black Mamba, there were very few players who declared early to enter the NBA draft. When he went straight from the gym of Lower Merion to the NBA stadiums, he became the first shooting guard, and only the third player in the history of basketball to bypass college. Before

Kobe, college players would stay in school for four years. Even the casual fan would know what players played for which school. The level of play was elite. But Bryant kicked open the door for the best college players to never step foot on the university. Following Kobe's trail, a flood of talented players went directly to the NBA. But apart from LeBron James and a select few, it was rare to enjoy success like Bryant. In what would become one of the great 'what ifs', many have wondered how things would be different today if Kobe went to college and played for Coach K at Duke. If he went to college, he would have chosen to become a Blue Devil, because he wanted to learn the game from a great coach.

During Phil Jackson's first Laker's training camp (October 1999), Phil Jackson taught Kobe, Shaq and the Lakers the famed triangle offense. Kobe, one of the smartest basketball players of all time, quickly processed the intricacies of the offense. When Phil Jackson was announced as the Lakers coach, Kobe immediately did a deep dive to master the complicated triangle schemes. His teammates simply did not match Kobe's intellect and drive. After two weeks of bumps, bruises and painfully slow learning at training camp, Kobe turned on his teammates. He yelled out in anger, "Did any of you guys get TNT?" (The Bulls were on television so much in the 90s, Kobe had completely mastered the offense by simply watching the games.) As Kobe thought about how dull his teammates were, his only possible conclusion was that they didn't have cable tv growing up!

In Phil Jackson's first month as Kobe's coach, he told Kobe he was too young and too arrogant and he must change his attitude for the sake of the team. During that first training camp, Jackson laid out his vision for the team, "Every great team has a one-two punch. This is your team, Shaq. And Kobe, you're gonna be our floor leader. If you guys don't like that, let me know now and I'll trade you tomorrow. You're gonna do what I say, and if you don't, you're out of here." Shaquille, not Kobe, would be the center and foundation of the 2000-2004 Lakers teams. So Phil built a strong relationship with 'The Big Diesel' and intentionally ignored the younger superstar. Kobe talked to no one on the team, talked mad trash during practices, and would even become violent with teammates. The day Kobe shared a meal with a teammate it made heads turn. He left the triangle offense to pad his stats. His teammates hated that he never passed the ball to the open man. The frustration was real. O'Neal, Fisher, Horry, and Fox even came up with a hand signal— a downward twitch of the thumb—which would freeze Bryant out. When a player made the signal, no one would pass the ball to Kobe. Bryant never caught on. During his first years with the Lakers, Jackson met one-on-one with Shaq each week. Kobe Bryant requested similar meetings. His requests were flat out denied for two years. Phil Jackson ignored Kobe and never met with him personally because he never wanted Shaq to feel threatened by his relationship with Bryant.

Although the mentoring relationship was cold and severe, Phil Jackson knew that Bryant was a truly elite player. He had never seen the combination of talent, knowledge, competitive drive that so naturally flowed out of Kobe, in anyone else, except for Michael Jordan. At the height of their team conflicts in 2001, the Detroit Pistons offered to trade Grant Hill to the Lakers for Kobe Bryant. Many in the organization urged Phil to sign off on the deal. They tried to convince Phil that his life would be easier, team chemistry would be better, and with Hill they could still win titles. But Jackson's competitive side took over and he rejected the deal because Bryant was six years younger and his ceiling was higher.

When compared to Dean Smith, Phil Jackson had considerable flaws and weaknesses. All of his peers chastised him when he broke the unwritten rule of openly campaigning for another man's job. Del Harris was still the coach of the Lakers when Phil Jackson began dropping less than subtle hints in the media that he was interested in coaching Shaq and Kobe. Jerry Krause, the general manager of the Chicago Bulls, went so far as to warn his counterpart with the Lakers, Jerry West, "Stay away from Phil Jackson. He is trouble. He is manipulative and he is mean!"

Dr. Jerry Buss hired Jackson, against the wishes of Jerry West.

Within months, Jackson, who had recently divorced his wife of twenty-four years, was dating Jeannie Buss, the owner's daughter. He famously yelled expletives at West after a playoff game for entering the Lakers locker room at Staples Center. The general manager who recruited and signed free-agent Shaquille O'Neal and engineered the drafting of Kobe Bryant, was suddenly banished from the locker room of the men he said were like his children. Thus began the power play that resulted in 'The Logo' being exiled from the purple and gold. And somehow, through all of the highs and lows of this ultradramatic environment, Jackson did with Bryant what he did with Jordan. He helped Kobe Bryant become a champion.

Phil Jackson was the primary teacher who helped Bryant fulfill his destiny.

JESUS OF NAZARETH

No man ever spoke like Jesus. He made audacious claim after audacious claim to help the world see that He was no man. The book of John is the fourth biographical account of Jesus' words and deeds. The author was Jesus' best friend. John, the Son of Zebedee, was a fishermen from Galilee when Jesus walked up to his boat and changed his life. Inspired by the Holy Spirit, he penned a statement of incarnation that captures the reason why Jesus is easily the greatest teacher in the world. No man has ever seen God, but the only begotten Son of God, He has made Him known (John 1:18).

No human being has ever seen God. That does not mean He isn't real or present in our lives through the Holy Spirit. None of us has ever seen the wind, but we feel it against our face and we see it's power as trees bend when it blows. No one in the history of the world can say that they have seen God but Jesus has made Him known. How did the carpenter make God known to the world? Jesus was with God in the beginning and Jesus was God from the beginning (John 1:1). As we experience the Christian life, we realize that at the center of the universe is a relationship. The Father, the Son and the Holy Spirit are a family love affair since before the world was created. Jesus was before the beginning, and at the appointed time, in His great love for us, He became one of us. He went on to say, "If you have seen me, you have seen my Father (John 14:9)." No man has ever spoken like Jesus. Because he is no mere man.

Do you ever wonder what God is like? If so, then you just need to look at Jesus. He is like God in every single way because He is God, come to earth, in human form. When we look at Jesus' life, we realize that God is amazing, beautiful, loving, and the Father that we have always wanted (and needed). Because we see Jesus, we know that the Father goes to weddings and turns water into wine (John 2:1-11). Because we see Jesus, we know that the Father flips over corrupt religious systems that stop people from experiencing his love (John 2:12-25). Because we see Jesus we know He offers water to the spiritually thirsty (John 4:13) and He provides heavenly bread for the spiritually hungry (John 6:35). And because we see Jesus, we know that demons scream when He enters a room, children play in his lap, and when He screamed "It is finished" as He breathed his last breathe on the cross, the history of the world changed forever (John 19:30).

Simply put, Jesus is the greatest teacher of all time. Who else would leave heaven for the sake of the creatures He made from dust? Who else would forever put away His spirit form to forever be chained to our human frames? Who else would suffer and die for sinners who have blasphemed His holy name? No man has ever spoken like Jesus. And no man has ever done the deeds that filled Jesus' life and ministry.

DO YOU NEED ANY BREAD?

John's Gospel highlights seven signs that Jesus performed. We like to define what is often a mysterious and miraculous concept in the day to day in our own lives. Think about how difficult life would be if there were no signs. A sign is an experience, a statement or information shared that points to a greater, unseen reality. For example, let's say you are driving at a normal speed around a blind corner. But suddenly you notice a bright yellow sign that tells you a school is just around the bend and there may be children crossing the street. Without the sign you would not know that the school was there. But the sign points to a greater, unseen reality. When signs are understood and we process the information, our lives begin to change. Because you see and understand the sign, you take your foot off the gas and drive with more caution, for the sake of the little pedestrians that may be crossing to the other side.

In the same way, Jesus performed signs to teach us about the greater, unseen reality of the Kingdom of God. One of His most famous signs involved bread. He was teaching a massive crowd of **5000 people**. The people listened to Him teach as they sat on a rural hill. This was not the United Center where they could easily rise from their seats and buy a killer Chicago hot dog. Jesus was given five barley loaves and two fish from a little boy (we know it was barley loaves because the author was an eyewitness to the great sign). Jesus prayed to His Father and God multiplied the bread, feeding all 5000 people with only five loaves. True story!

How do I (JT) know it's true? Because the exact same sign happened to me. Before I became the pastor of Fountain of Life Covenant Church, I worked as a campus minister at USC. The wealthy, elite and powerful campus is located right in the middle of South Central. My wife and I have a big heart for the poor. Jesus the Teacher has taught us so much through our friends who often find themselves in tough situations. It was my regular practice to expose often wealthy and privileged college students to the amazing people who lived on the streets. Every Tuesday night for three years I would bring students with me to feed, clothe, and pray for my friends who lived in cardboard boxes on Skid Row.

When you enter Skid Row you are immediately greeted with the smell of urine and drugs. Hundreds of people line the street living inside their cardboard shelter. I was very intimidated at first, but after a while I became friends with many of the people who lived there. After Bible study one night we arrived at Skid Row around 9PM. A large crowd began lining up. Because it was a warm night not many went into the shelters. There were roughly 300 people lined up.

About half way through our line, Beth Anne from Pasadena,

looked at me frantically. She was in the peanut butter and jelly sandwich line. They were cranking out sandwiches, with peanut butter flying everywhere. She made eye contact with me and said, "John, we have run out of bread." I wonder if Beth Anne knew that she was literally quoting the disciples before Jesus fed the hungry 5000. Just like the disciples on the mountain that day, there were no other options. At Skid Row there are no Subway, Jersey Mikes or bacon-wrapped hot dog stands. The nearest market was 15 minutes away. We were going to have to shut down the feeding line. But then I felt in my spirit that God would do something special.

Thirty seconds later the sign from God became clear. An old Lincoln Continental town car pulled up behind my little Honda Civic. (There are literally no cars that drive through Skid Row this late in the evening). A short Latino man jumped out of his car, looked me in the eye and said, "Do you need any bread?"

My mouth hit the ground. My tongue was tied. But I managed to ask a silly question, "Are you a baker?" He said, "No! I'm a shoe repair man. Come on over." He then opened up his trunk, which was filled with two Hefty bags full of loaves of bread. I was shocked. He then told me his side of the sign. "I am a shoe repair man in El Monte (20 minutes from Skid Row). A bakery is next to me and at the end of the day the owner gave me her two extra bags full of loaves. I stopped and prayed to God. The Holy Spirit told me to drive down tonight to Skid Row to make the delivery. So, do you need any bread or what?"

And just like as in the original sign over 2,000 years ago, we passed out all the bread until everyone ate their fill. After ministry was complete, we gathered together to count the loaves. There were 10 loaves left over (9 students and me). Just like the original disciples of Jesus, everyone of us received our own loaf (John 6:13).

I learned such an important lesson that night. While there are many teachers in this world, there is no one like Jesus. No one talked like Him, no one lived like Him, and certainly no one else performed miraculous signs like Him. The world is full of teachers but I want to shout from the roof tops that there is simply no one like Jesus. Who else gets involved in our lives so personally and so powerfully?

As we close this chapter, we would like to invite you into a faith challenge. Would you take a moment to think about your life? Where have you run out of bread? Will you take a small step of faith and pray the following prayer?

"Lord Jesus, when I look inside my soul or outside at what's going on, I confess to you that I am hungry. I want to eat some of your hidden food. Will you please give me some of your living bread?"

Jesus is not only the great Teacher. He is also the great provider and loves to feed His friends.

Do you need any bread?

SOUL DYNAMICS

● **BIBLE**

No one has ever seen God; the only God, who is at the Father's side, he has made him known. (John 1:18)

● **REFLECTION**

(1) Who are the teachers who have most shaped your life?
(2) Have you ever read the teachings of Jesus and his invitation to become your central teacher?

● **PRAYER**

Jesus, please give me a fresh sign to show me how great a Teacher you truly are!

5

RACE

At the bottom of our news tonight,
there's been a new animal aimed at
falling off the face of our Earth.
Yes, young Black teenagers are reported to be
the oldest, and the newest, creatures added
to the endangered species list.
As of now, no efforts have been made to
preserve the Blacks. When asked why,
a top law official adds,
"Because they make good game."

'ENDANGERED SPECIES'
ICE CUBE
FT. FEMALE NEWS REPORTER

JORDAN, BRYANT AND RACE

From Biblical times to today, our world continues to fight one of the oldest viruses that has plagued our culture: racism. When we were boys there were very few truly transcendent African-American sports role models. Jackie Robinson must be considered in any conversation as the most impactful Black athlete in the history of America. The personal suffering he endured, and his strength of character to overcome the color barrier in baseball, is truly legendary. There is a reason that every single team in Major League Baseball has retired the iconic number 42. And then there's Muhammed Ali, who was not only the greatest boxer who ever lived (sorry Mike Tyson fans), but also a champion for personal freedom. He was one of the first Black athletes to stand up in the face of dominant and racist American culture and proclaim, "I will do things my way." In addition, Arthur Ashe must be considered one of the most significant Black athletes. Ashe peaked as the number two tennis player in the world. Today, he is the only Black man to ever win Wimbledon, the Australian Open, and the U.S. Open. Sadly, he left us too soon as he died from AIDS, contracted from a blood transfusion gone really bad. And to those who study the man, his writings far outlive his prolific tennis career.

There are countless others, known and unknown who paved the way for Jordan. But as noted in our chapter on destiny, a seismic shift occurred in 1984. With the convergence of cable television, a lawyer turned NBA commissioner who was gifted in marketing, and a truly magnetic basketball player and person, Michael Jordan shattered every ceiling that once held back Black athletes. Jordan has achieved levels of worldly success as an African-American athlete that would have been dismissed as pure fiction only a generation before. Chris Rock once joked about the difference between being rich and wealthy. The rich man has money. The wealthy man has big money. "Shaquille O'Neal signed a $100 million contract. He's rich. But Dr. Buss paid him $100 million. He's wealthy." It is not lost on anyone that in 25 years Michael Jordan climbed the sporting world's Mount Everest, becoming the first former player to become the controlling owner of an NBA franchise.

Jordan thoughtfully constructed a platform that grew and grew and grew into a global empire. Endorsements from Nike, Gatorade, Hanes, Coca-Cola, McDonald's and Wheaties skyrocketed his influence across the planet. It was not only Jordan's talent that inspired his vast audience, but it was his steely character, insatiable drive and maniacal dedication that made everyone sing, 'I want to be like Mike.' Michael Jordan established a pop culture baseline for respect, dignity and equality for Black people in America, and all across the planet.

It cannot be understated what an ethnic superstar does for the next generation from those cultures. Seeing your own race on the biggest stages brings a new perspective. Seeing one of your own holding the trophy creates new dreams. For those from the minority cultures, role models who look like you inspire one to dig deeper and work harder and somehow believe it could happen for you as well. Who can forget the joy and pride of Asians across the world when Michael Chang at age 17 won the 1989 French Open? Mexican-Americans will forever treasure how Fernando-mania swept Los Angeles and Major League Baseball in 1980. Chang and Valenzuela not only dominated tennis and baseball, but became shining stars of the Asian- American and Mexican-American communities as global sports heroes.

It must be noted that Jordan was by no means perfect in regards to race relationships. Early in his career, Jordan chose profits over people. He was asked to stand up to Jesse Helms, an overtly racist senator from his home state who was running against Harvey Gantt. Jordan famously quipped that he would not endorse the African-American candidate because "Republicans buy sneakers too." This theme of choosing profits over people continued when a scandalous report emerged that Nike was paying sweatshop workers $1 a day to manufacture Air Jordans in a Bangkok, Thailand sweatshop. The same shoe was then shipped to America and sold for $150. When confronted with this injustice after a regular season game Jordan said, "I will definitely look into this…once the playoffs are finished." No one ever heard of what came of Jordan's personal investigation of the child labor incident.

Bryant was far more vocal than his idol in regards to standing up against racism and injustice. He used his media platform for change (we have no doubt MJ's social media game would have been immaculate had he been a mega-star in this era). Throughout his career, Kobe Bean made it a point to add his commentary on social issues. In 2014, Eric Garner was brutally killed while in the custody of the police. "I can't breathe" was exclaimed 11 times before he ultimately suffocated to death. Shortly after Garner's death, Bryant organized for the Lakers to take the court wearing t-shirts with Garner's last words written boldly across their chests.

Bryant's voice was stronger than Jordan's not only because of generational differences, but because of Kobe's global upbringing. When the Bryants moved to Italy, Kobe was a six year old boy. He said he could never 'unhear' all he heard at the European soccer matches flung at Black players. He gives credit to his parents for teaching him how to battle racism with education and experience.

As we consider so many of our cities today, is it a stretch to argue that the uniting of races around the game of basketball are among Jordan and Bryant's greatest achievements? They brought entire cities together. Playing for the Bulls and the Lakers, these two legends became driving forces uniting people no matter what race, class, gender, age, or socio-economic background. When Kobe and Michael won titles and crowds poured out of the United Center and Staples Center the entire city rejoiced. CEOs and gang-bangers would straight hug it out.

On a recent trip to a small mountain town called Mammoth, I (John) went to the grocery store to pick up a few things. I was wearing my Black Mamba sweatshirt. As I went to pick up a gallon of milk, a Latino man shopping with his children stopped me and said, "Wow! That is a cool sweatshirt." On another aisle a young Asian teen was shopping with his mother. He had a Mamba Mentality sweatshirt. We didn't say a word to each other but low key nodded in respect. I could go on and on, sharing story after story, about how the Lakers gold 24 jersey and the Kobe sneaker game bring black, brown, yellow, and white together. Jordan and Bryant possessed a unique ability to unify across painful divides. And in this divided world, racism far too often has the last word.

BEING BLACK IN AMERICA

My (PMT) hometown of Chicago, a place I love and will always love, is hugely segregated. This division was the diseased fruit of many generations of racist, fearful and self-serving leaders. Sadly racism attacks whenever it pleases, rearing it's ugly head to bring pain, shame, fear, and profound frustration all in it's path. Even children. I will never forget a traumatic experience my wife, oldest son Jeremiah (barely one year old at the time), and I went through while navigating the streets of Chicago. I was driving as our family was rolling to get some dinner after a church service. This was a special service at our church so I was still in my clergy collar and suit. We were driving through a well-known racist neighborhood but I thought we could get a quick meal and then bounce. One thing Black people know all too well, is the level of awareness we are required to have when being outside of our homes, especially driving. I was on high alert as we rolled through the well documented racist hood. I was straight 10-2 on the wheels, I made sure I was going the speed limit, and even though I was the poster-child for the next 'student driver video' the police car behind me flashed the berries and cherries and pulled me over.

With my wife and baby boy in his car seat in the back, I immediately drove the car to the side of the street. You always have to ask the time of the year in Chicago. The wind starts howling off Lake Michigan in November and the snow follows close behind. It was December in Chicago, and the weather that day was in the single digits. Without any probable cause, the popo demanded we all get out of the car and sit on the street curb. My wife and I were furious, because of the way we were being treated and the clear lack of concern for our baby boy in extreme weather. We were also very afraid because we all know far too well how this common story often plays out. We bit our tongue, suppressed our anger, and complied with those in authority over us. The emotion that called out for anger was quickly gobbled up by the powerful instinct to survive. We showed restraint.

The officers claimed our car matched a description of a car that was known for dealing drugs. I wanted to call him out and ask him if he has ever seen people driving around dealing drugs from out of their car. All I can think of is Big Perm in 'Friday' who dealt out of the ice cream truck. All the drug dealers I knew lived in the dark corners and people came to them. But I chose another path. I shared with the officer that I was a minister and there was no way we were who they were allegedly looking for. In return, he demanded that we follow them to the police station where he proceeded to fingerprint me. After many grueling hours I was finally released.

Because of my church affiliation and access to attorneys through Operation PUSH, I found out about an ongoing process where police wrongfully created scenarios of getting Black men's fingerprints to put them into the system. I eventually had those illegally obtained fingerprints removed, but the trauma Kim, Jeremiah and I went through could never be removed.

While I was grateful to know people who helped me and my family throughout this ordeal, I was heartbroken thinking about all of the other young brothers who simply endured racist and criminal activity from those who have sworn to serve and protect. I was so distraught. And yet, I was able to maintain hope.

Why?

Because I knew that my Jesus knew exactly what it was like to be me, to be Black. The Jesus of the Bible is not the Hollywood Jesus from the 1990s films. He did not have Swedish blonde hair and light blue swimming pool eyes. No, the Creator of the world chose to become human and live as a dark-skinned Palestinian Jew. He was not born in the wing of the hospital named after his father. He was born in a feeding trough with a stable fully of stanky animals. He did not grow up on the elite banks of Lake Michigan, he grew up in a run down hood named Nazareth. This city is to the Ancient Mediterranean world what some of the toughest cities today are to America. Isn't it interesting how you just say the name of the city and people will react: South Side, Compton, Bronx? One of Jesus' own racist disciples openly ridiculed his humble beginnings, "Can anything good come out of Nazareth?" (John 1:46). Jesus should have dropped the mix-tape 'Straight Outta Nazareth!' Jesus, the dark-skinned Savior, knew exactly what me and my family went through, and continue to battle.

Being Black in America is both beautiful and terrifying. We are a people who live in perpetual trauma and yet, God has blessed us in such a rich way to still be tribal, love family and community, and in the words of Beyonce, 'make lemonade!' To be Black and still drop 55 points in The Garden, to be Black and still drop 81 points on Toronto, to be Black and still live our lives with the dignity of being a child of God. I look at the patient endurance and the quiet strength of Black Christians and I see the personal and powerful presence of the Holy Spirit. Our very lives are proof that Jesus can give you a deep-seated joy in him that the world didn't give and therefore the world cannot take away. It's a joy that doesn't blind you to the injustices we see, but compels you to fight injustice because you are able to hold onto a joy in this world that is worth fighting for.

I wish I could tell you that being a senior pastor exempted me from this harsh reality. But that is simply not true. Racism is no respecter of persons, lashing out at whoever and whenever it pleases.While we are headed in the right direction, there are dimensions of MLK's dream — that people would be judged, not on the color of their skin but by the content of their character, that have yet to be realized. And we continue to eat the diseased fruit of racism and racial profiling primarily targeting to Black, Brown and Asian people.

We must understand that in a country filled with so many racist people and protocols, whether you're an NBA champion or a minister driving home from church on a cold winter afternoon, or even a carpenter from Nazareth, the reality is when you are Black, people will often assume the worst about you. And when you are White, even on your worst day, you will be treated with greater dignity and respect. This is the linchpin reality that continues to keep us segregated. And it will take faithful pioneers to undo centuries of ignorant thinking and violent oppressions. How we will emerge stronger and follow God into a better world for our children?

The answer is love.

RACE & MARRIAGE

My (JT) mother was born in 1928 in Korea. My grand-parents did not meet each other until their wedding day. A matchmaker arranged the marriage in a traditional Korean way. My Mom and Dad met on August 5, 1954. Mom boarded a steam ship named 'Choctau' that was traveling from Seattle to Seoul. My father, a Dutch man from Mobile, Alabama, was the third mate on the ship. He played baseball in college so I like to call him a Seattle Mariner. My dad was smoove and asked my Mom to teach him the Korean language. During the three week trip (may we never complain about air travel again) Paul and Yung Soon fell in love. My mother stayed in Seoul and my father had to return to Seattle. For six months, he wrote a letter almost every single day. He came to Seoul in January 1955 to propose. I like to think that Dad held Mom as she spread her arms over the bow of the ship and screamed out "I'm the king of the world!" This is my vision of a 'Multi-ethnic Titanic.'

Mom was now 26 years old but still needed the traditional Korean seal for marriage. Her father had died a few years earlier during the Korean War. And my Korean grandmother was not interested in her daughter marrying an American man. When Paul arrived to announce his intention to marry Yung Soon, my Grandmother dropped a bomb on him, "For 4,288 years (lunar calendar) the Whang family has been pure Korean blood. We have no Mongolian, no Chinese, nor Japanese. Now, we are not going to have a 'Kojooboo' (this is a derogatory insult which Koreans use to identify westerners) in our family!" My mom said she was heartbroken and apologized to my dad. My father stood his ground and in front of grandmother and my five future uncles, he calmly said, "With all due respect, we are adults and we are in love. I did not come here to ask for Yung Soon's hand in marriage. I came to here to share our intentions." Mom and Dad married on April 23, 1955 in Seoul, Korea.

When my Mom became engaged this caused quite a stir at the woman's university. My mother was an English professor and was very popular among the students. The dean called her into her office and asked her if the rumors were true, "Are you engaged to an American?" My mom quickly affirmed that she was engaged to Paul Teter. Her supervisor then declared this was a mistake and set a very bad example for the young women. Mom was given two options: call off the engagement or quit her professorship immediately. My mom thought about it and spoke with her mother who wanted her to stay in Korea. She decided to call off the engagement.

As she walked into the dean's office to tell the dean that she was calling off the engagement, the dean's assistant made a snarky comment about Paul Teter. My mom was indignant, pulled out a sheet of paper and wrote her resignation letter on the spot. Love overcame hate. And it is truly amazing to me how I would not be here today if the dean's assistant could have controlled her tongue.

Whether the context is your own Korean home in the 1950s, a university where you are employed as one of the most popular professors, or the South Side of Chicago driving home from a Sunday worship service, racism is real. Each of us, and our family members before, to greater or lesser degrees have had to learn to live in a world where opposing races answer Rodney King's forever looming question, "Can't we all get along?" Without God's help, the answer is clearly no.

With great hope, we cannot wait to introduce you to the most inspiring church in the Bible to understand God's will for race relations.

ANTIOCH & GOD'S MULTI-ETHNIC FAMILY

Did you know that two of the greatest books of the New Testament, 'The Gospel of Luke' (the clearest historical account of Jesus' life and ministry) and 'Acts of the Apostles' (the clearest history of how the church began) were written by a Black man? The author is Lucius of Cyrene (Acts 13:1). Luke is a nickname for Lucius. He was a physician, church planter, theologian and author. He was from Cyrene, Northern Africa. He is the only Gentile author in the New Testament. We often run into people who are not familiar with their Biblical history and because of historical sins, mainstream and social media, they falsely declare that Christianity is a White man's religion. Nothing could be further from the truth. Not only was Jesus from the Middle East and rocked the dark skin, but one of the founding evangelists was a distinguished physician from Africa. The very beginnings of God's plan for the world centered on Black people!

We take great hope in the first multi-ethnic church. It began by accident as two faithful but nameless Hebrew brothers shared their faith with people outside of their race. The Lord blessed that **evangelism** and Luke writes that a great number believed and turned to the Lord (Acts 11:20-21). Up to this point the church was only Hebrew people. There would be people from different countries but they were all Jewish. This was the first truly **multi-ethnic church**. And boy did they do church! They studied the Bible together. They sang worship songs to God together. They took care of each other when they were sick or in need. And they sacrificially loved their city together. The ancient city of Antioch was marvelous and overflowed with luxury. There were four quarters (very similar to the city of New Orleans today). The four quarters were: Syrian, Greek, Roman, and Hebrew. Each quarter had its own distinct culture, values and customs. People did not cross the line to engage in multi-ethnic activity. In the infamous words of Lavar Ball, 'everybody stayed in their lane.'

But the Christians were straight different. The love of God brought all of these races together. The new family of God exploded in love for one another and the city was shocked. They had no idea what could bring these races together. They were drawn to the love that they saw in people who should hate each other. The loving work of God to make different people spiritual brothers and sisters not only baffled, but intrigued the city. It is noteworthy that it was in Antioch that the disciples of Jesus were first called Christians. The first Christians did not name themselves. They were named by the great city because there was no other way to describe this united group!

THOMAS AND TETER FAMILY

At this point, some of us might be skeptical. We live in such a divided and segregated world. In so many ways the last five years of American culture (2016-2021) have gashed and gouged wounds that have caused so many people to retreat into friendship circles of people who look, think, and act just like them. We fear that it will take years and years for our country to heal. But just like He did in the city of Antioch, Jesus today is tearing down **dividing walls of hostility** (Ephesians 2:14) that the **devil** uses to segregate and separate the races. When you become a Christian, race certainly still matters, but you experience a quality of spiritual family that far transcends human race and culture.

Ray Bakke is a famous preacher and he explained this best. Ray and his wife ministered in the inner-city of Chicago for over 30 years. When his son, Brian went to kindergarten he became best friends with another Brian. Ray's son was White and his best friend was Black. The young boy tragically lost his parents in the second grade. With no one to take care of the boy, Ray and his wife adopted the boy. Ray suddenly had two seven year old sons both named Brian. One was White and one was Black. The both loved each other so much and had so much fun together. Ray said that being in the same family not only helped them understand race but also focus on all they had in common. The boys said it best when they ran into Ray's study one morning screaming, "Daddy, we are different colors but our poop is the same color!"

The Thomas and Teter families have become intertwined. God first brought us together in 2013 at a pastors conference in San Diego, CA. Over the years we enjoyed each other but in 2016 the Lord intensified our friendship. Today, we support one another, encourage one another, and we truly love one another. Our children play tennis together, watch movies together, clown each other on FaceTime, celebrate big birthdays and milestones together and our families vacation together. And now we write together. And you know we watch lots and lots of basketball together.

God has broken down the dividing wall of hostility and we have become brothers in every way. This is one of the greatest benefits of being citizens in the **Kingdom of God**. We must become the change agents in the world, shining a radiant light in our dark and broken world. True change will only come when our hearts are changed and we submit to the ways of Jesus. The world's way only promotes vengeance; Jesus' way promotes justice. The world's system will not last, it will still produce a formula that ends with one side winning at the expense of the other side losing. But the way of Christ will empower us to take our allotted place, atop the scorer's table, raising our hands in victory of racism and injustice.

We may be different colors, but our poop is the same.

We may be different colors, but our sin is the same.

We may be different colors, but the precious blood that forgives us is the same.

SOUL DYNAMICS

● **BIBLE**

For He Himself is our peace, who has made us both one and has broken down in His flesh the dividing wall of hostility. (Ephesians 2:14)

● **REFLECTION**

Where do you need Jesus to touch you and bring racial healing in your life?

● **PRAYER**

Jesus, will you please touch me and bless me to be a peacemaker and reconciler in this dark and divided world.

6

LOSS

There's a time that I remember,
when I did not know no pain
When I believed in forever,
and everything would stay the same
Now my heart feel like December
when somebody say your name

'MEMORIES'
MAROON 5

THE CRASH

On January 31, 2020, the Los Angeles Lakers hosted the Portland Trailblazers at Staples Center. This was game 49 of the season and the Blazers took down the Lakers behind Dame Lillard's 48 points. But the box score does not capture the meaning of that night. Kobe and Gianna Bryant had died in a tragic helicopter accident five days before.

On January 26, 2020, Kobe Bryant and his thirteen-year-old daughter, Gigi Bryant, died. Kobe Bryant had launched the Mamba Sports Academy a few years earlier, housed in Thousand Oaks, California although Bryant and his family lived 65 miles south in Newport Coast. That fateful Sunday morning Kobe, Gigi and seven other passengers boarded a Sikorsky S-76B helicopter at 9:06 AM. The flight plan was John Wayne Airport to Camarillo Airport. The flight was much easier than the 90+ minute drive from Newport to Thousand Oaks. Kobe was scheduled to coach Gianna's team later in the morning. But they left earlier so they could scout another team they might have faced at a later round in the tournament.

In Southern California, the marine layer can become very thick in the morning hours. Flight records showed that vision was impaired, manual flight controls compromised, and the luxury helicopter clipped a hillside at 9:45 AM while at 1,085 feet. Ditching was inevitable and all nine occupants died immediately upon impact.

Isaac Flores and I (JT) arrived early at Staples Center that night. Mourners packed the entire LA Live area. Barricade check points were established. Only those with team credentials or game tickets were permitted behind the barrier. The normal festive pre-game atmosphere was gone. A dark sad cloud filled the air. Isaac and I entered through the press and media area. We stood a few feet from Jalen Rose, Stephen A. Smith and the ESPN basketball crew as they tearfully processed the tragic loss.

Thirty minutes before the game, the entire Staples Center bowl was packed. In a rare moment for Los Angeles sports fans, everyone was in their seat 30 minutes before tip off. LA fans are notorious for arriving late. I have only seen the bowl filled this early two other times: Christmas Day 2004 when Shaq returned for the first time as a villain (recently traded to the Miami Heat). The other time was Game 7 of the 2010 NBA Finals against the Boston Celtics, a game which many consider the single greatest basketball game ever played.

As I walked around the arena, everyone had heavy hearts and swollen eyes. Total strangers spoke in hushed tones. I spoke to a stranger who shared what Kobe meant to his teenage boy. Another stranger opened up about how Kobe's loss triggered her own traumatic loss. I shared a moment with one of the owners of the Milwaukee Brewers, who wore his "LOVE" shirt from the Mamba Day retirement game. Standing next to his own son he offered thoughtful reflection on fathers and loss. That night 18,799 people in Staples Center were united in suffering.

As I made my way to the north end of the arena, moments before the players emerged from the tunnel, Rob Pelinka, general manager of the Lakers, and Kobe's best friend, walked by me. He shared a tearful embrace with Dr. Patrick Soong-Shiong, one of the owners of the Lakers. He is a surgeon and carefully navigated Kobe through his Achilles repair and recovery. DeMarcus Cousins cried behind the bench. Matt Barnes wept as he hugged ESPN reporter Ramona Shelburne. Lawrence Tanter, the Lakers public address announcer, repeated the same introduction he speaks before every game, "Now, taking the floor, your Los Angeles Lakers." When the players run out onto the floor, hype music fills the entire arena. The production team seems to always pick the right song to begin the night. As Lawrence welcomed our heartbroken team, I wondered what hype song would be played that night.

As the Lakers took the floor, Kendrick Lamar's 'Alright' blasted throughout Staples Center.

The song is about hope in the midst of suffering, pain and loss. The context of this urban hymn is police brutality. It proved to be a prophetic warning as Derek Chauvin's brutal murder of George Floyd in Minneapolis would take place in a few short months. As Kendrick sang the line, 'We gon' be alright' over and over, it somehow perfectly captured the moment. I looked around at the crowd. They wanted to believe the song they were singing. They wanted to be strong. They wanted to be resilient in the face of devastating loss. And they wanted to believe the future was not random.

"Do you hear me?"

"Do you feel me?"

"We gon' be alright!"

The Lakers took the court wearing Kobe Bryant jerseys. Anthony Davis, mentored by Kobe since the 2012 Olympics, had tears streaming down his face. LeBron James, Kobe's equal in every way, wiped away his tears as he stood in the lay up line. It turns out that in a simple twist of fate, Kobe's last social media post was giving LeBron love for passing him and moving into third on the all-time NBA scoring leaders list.

I was forty feet from center court filming Usher as he sang the great Christian hymn, "Amazing Grace." Ben Hong, a Los Angeles Philharmonic cellist, and no stranger to traumatic loss himself, struck the perfect note as he performed "Hallelujah," bathing Staples in beauty as our hearts were full of grief and sadness. LeBron took center court, tore up his notes and spoke from his heart. He honored his fallen friend. Boys to Men, rocking Mamba 8/24 shirts, blessed the basketball hero from their hometown of Philly by singing the national anthem.

"Do you hear me?"

"Do you feel me?"

"We gon' be alright!"

JAMES JORDAN

One would think that conquering the world would make you exempt from the sufferings of the common man or woman. But that is not true. Suffering is a respecter of no people and when he brings his dark cloud over your life, he could care less if you are CEO, soccer mom, elementary school teacher, or even a global NBA icon. It has been said that death is the great equalizer. This is certainly true not only for Kobe, but for MJ as well.

On July 23, 1993, James Jordan was murdered. Michael Jordan's father's red Lexus was found near Fayetteville, North Carolina, stripped and shattered. His body was recovered 60 miles away next to a creek in a shallow lake near McColl, South Carolina. It appears that Jordan was driving home to Wilmington late one evening. He was tired and instead of powering through the long drive, he stopped on the side of a North Carolina highway to sleep for the night. Lawrence Martin Deremy, age 17, and Daniel Andre Green, age 18, were troubled youth with criminal records. Records show they used James Jordan's phone that night, linking them to the death. They were arrested for carjacking and the murder of Michael Jordan's father. Both were found guilty by the court and were handed 25 with an L for the senseless murder of a man sleeping on the side of a road.

To inflict even more pain, the media went out of their way to link the deaths to Michael Jordan's gambling activity. Instead of reporting the event as an isolated incident, stories all over the nation began to pop up that the mob was behind this because Jordan refused to pay gambling debts. These stories have never been proven. In the documentary, 'The Last Dance' it was mentioned that how the media handled the death of his father caused Michael to pull back. What had once been a warm and mutually beneficial relationship suddenly soured never to regain that warmth.

MJ loved his father. His tragic death devastated Michael Jordan. Throughout his time on the Bulls, Jordan was always known as a communicator. He might have been harsh on certain teammates and unnecessarily mean to others, but he was always talking. Steve Kerr's segment on fathers during the 'The Last Dance' captured the depths of Jordan's pain. Kerr lost his own father to a senseless shooting in Beirut. The elder Kerr was president of a university and during the political upheaval, he was kidnapped and murdered. What are the odds that two of the seven rotation players on the 1996-1999 Chicago Bulls would both have fathers who were murdered? When asked how often Kerr and Jordan discussed their sufferings, Kerr replied, "We never talked about it once."

Two months after the murder, 23 shocked the sports world and retired from the Chicago Bulls. He had just won three straight titles, something no NBA basketball team had achieved since games were on black and white television. Jordan reflected shortly after the death of his father, "This has made me realize how short life is and how quickly things can end." Jordan's father always loved baseball. So MJ decided to honor his father by becoming a professional baseball player.

SUFFERING & GOD'S PROMISE TO WORK

As pastors, we have the incredible honor of being God's ambassador for the highest of highs in the human experience: weddings, baby dedications, and baptism. There is truly nothing like standing next to a man when the doors of the church open and he sees his bride walking down the aisle. But as pastors, we also carry the incredible responsibility of being God's ambassador for the lowest of lows in life: broken relationships, divorce, job loss, sickness, and death. There is truly nothing like standing at the head of the casket with a family as they say good-bye to beloved family.

As pastors we are asked many questions about the faith. The questions usually resemble one of these questions: (1) How can you know the Bible is true? (2) Don't all religions say the same thing? (3) Why is the church full of hypocrisy? (4) Why is God trying to squash my fun? To be honest, when those questions are asked, we have been around long enough to have prepared answers and often it satisfies the heart and mind. But the fifth question is altogether different. The fifth question breaks our hearts. The fifth question is: (1) Why does God allow suffering? When someone asks us that question it is not about the head, but the heart. When that question is asked, we do not speak and give our pat answer. We sit down and prepare to listen. We answer that question with a question, "What are you going through?" The pain that comes from suffering is overwhelming, often locking us up in chains of confusion, anger and hopelessness. Yet, God sends his people to encourage those who are broken-hearted. And we will often share a Bible verse that has proven true over and over again.

You may have heard of a man named **Paul**. He started his life as one of the future superstars of the Jewish religious world. He had every gifting, outstanding qualification, and was being trained for the highest levels of leadership. He was zealous for the Hebrew religion, even resorting to violence against the first followers of Jesus. He was responsible for the stoning death of Stephen, one of the church's most faithful disciples (Acts 7:58). But everything changed in an instant for Paul. He was traveling by horse to put more Christians in jail when the Lord Jesus broke through the thin veil that separates our current world from the heavenly world. He surrounded Paul with a bright, flashing light, temporarily blinding him. He spoke to him words of both love and correction and set him on the path of God. Paul was spiritually blind to Jesus but he began to see. He became the movement's greatest church planter. He went on to write 13 of the 27 books, penning 32% of the New Testament. God inspired him to write this incredible promise to the church at Rome:

And we know that for those who love God all things work together for good, for those who are called according to his purpose. (Romans 8:28)

This promise sets the God of the Bible apart from every other religious leader in every other world religion. In this sacred text, God promises to redeem our sufferings. The previous chapters of the book are filled with suffering. Some of the suffering is what happens to us, along with self inflicted spiritual wounds. So often we just can't get out of our own way with sin. But God doesn't rub our noses in it. Instead, He promises that if you are called according to his purpose, and therefore love him, he will work all things for good in your life. We love that He doesn't say He will work a few things for good. We love that He doesn't say He will work the good things for good. No, He will work all things for good, even the things that have happened that we never want to speak on again. He will work the pain that we never thought we would get through. He will work all of it, every last drop, for the good of His people. Jesus alone promises to give meaning to our suffering.

God is like a master painter. Our lives are the canvas. And when the colors are vibrant and beautiful and the work of art is a day at the beach, we are delighted to be under the careful care of this painter. But we live in a broken world. And just as the painting is coming together, a little gang member breaks into the art studio with his can of spray paint. He tags his gang name, his street and tries to make a name for himself right on our beautiful canvas. We cannot believe this has happened. How could the master painter allow this to happen?

But that is when the Master Painter separates himself from all the other painters. You see, all of the other artists would have to throw away the canvas and start new. But not our God! He is different! He is all about the rescue and He puts His unlimited power, skill and sovereign ability to work all for good on our behalf. As we mourn the dripping graffiti paint seemingly ruining the painting of our lives, He comes in and somehow works with the graffiti. The result is a painting that is more beautiful and the Master Painter is praised for his unique ability. All of the other artists are playing checkers. But our God is playing 4-D, multi-board, floating in space, chess.

Who else has ever promised to work all things for good for those who love Him?

WHY GOD RESCUES US

During the last month of my high school senior year, I (JT) went bodyboarding at Huntington Beach. The waves were massive that late afternoon: 12 foot faces and 14 foot backs. When the waves pound at Huntington Beach they break about 100 yards from the shore. This makes fighting the waves to catch the set very difficult. A treacherous current coursed under the waves that day.

As an 18 year old, I thought I was indestructible. I foolishly entered the water with my body board but no fins. That was my first mistake. After battling hard for fifteen minutes, I tried to duck dive a wave but was slammed from the crest of the wave onto the slick face. I landed on the water that looked like glass and began flipping like a rag doll under the power of the massive wave. I thought I dislocated my shoulder. I did two revolutions. I came up for air only to be smashed in the face by another wave. Disoriented, I worked to the top and gasped for breath. My rip cord snapped. My board was halfway to shore. I took a moment to rest as I tried to catch my breath. That was my second mistake. I was trapped inside a deadly rip current.

The current was extremely powerful and unusually wide. I was being sucked out to sea at a forty-five degree angle. I could barely see the shore. I tried to swim sideways. I tried to swim forward. But this only pulled me farther and farther out to sea. When I realized I was thirty yards behind the break of the waves, I began to panic. My body went into full adrenaline mode but I could not escape the underwater current. I started drinking salt-water, guzzling gulp after gulp. I thought this had to be a nightmare. But it was real life. I was drowning. And there was nothing I could do about it. Tears began flowing down my cheeks. I said to myself, "Today is the day I will die."

In total desperation, I prayed a one word prayer to God, "Help!"

Nothing happened. I continued to struggle. I thought of my mother who had lost her husband to a glider plane accident eight years earlier. She would never recover from losing her son as well. A few more minutes passed. I was exhausted. The ocean had won. This is how it would end for me. I was prepared to die.

Without warning, I suddenly heard someone yell, "Grab this!"

A lifeguard threw me his red buoy. I clutched it to my chest with both hands. Somehow, the lifeguard saw me and had come to rescue me. The lifeguard was an incredible swimmer. I joke that he was 'half-Phelps and half-dolphin.' In what seemed like a moment, he delivered me to the shore. I fell to my knees on the sand and began vomiting salt-water. I looked up to thank the lifeguard but he was gone. I could only see his outline running at a super human pace a few hundred yards down the shoreline. He filled out no paperwork. He asked me no questions. He never asked my name. He only spoke two words to me, "Grab this!" God rescued me by sending an angel in the form of a life guard.

Three years later, I became a disciple of Jesus of Nazareth. On the first year anniversary of my conversion (May 8, 1993), I was in my childhood home praying. I was in the Spirit and God brought to mind my near death experience. I broke down weeping. It pierced my soul how close I was to death and how deserving I was to spend a billion years in **hell**.

As I prayed, a question formed on my lips. I lifted my eyes to heaven and asked my Father, "God, what was your perspective when you saved me from drowning?" I sat quietly and waited for an answer. I had never asked God such an intimate question. And I certainly never stopped to listen for an answer. But I waited quietly. And then it happened. The Word of God came to me. It is hard to describe but I knew it was God. He was breaking through the thin veil with his still-small voice.

The Father told me to read Psalm 18:16-19. As a new Christian, I had never read this Psalm before. "Alleluia" formed on my lips as tears rolled down my cheeks. God rescued me because He delights in me.

He sent from on high, he took me;
he drew me out of many waters.
He rescued me from my strong enemy
and from those who hated me,
for they were too mighty for me.
They confronted me in the day of my calamity,
but the LORD was my support.
He brought me out into a broad place;
he rescued me
because he delighted in me. (Psalm 18:16-19)

We do not know what you have been through. But if you are reading this book, God is actively fighting your strong enemy. We do not know what you are currently going through. But if you are reading this book, we believe God is in the process of rescuing you. We fundamentally believe that the key to all of life is to be someone that God calls according to His purpose. How do you know if you are called? If you love him then you are called. You cannot love God without first being called by Him. Live out that call in your life, fall in love with God, and this majestic promise will be true for you.

Why has God rescued you all these years? Because he delights in you.

Why will God continue to rescue you ? Because he delights in you.

God is not neutral with you. He absolutely loves you and wants nothing more than to work all things for your good.

Your painting will turn out beautiful. Trust us!

Kendrick Lamar says it best: "We're messed up Homie, you're messed up.. But if God's got us, we gon' be alright!"

SOUL DYNAMICS

- **BIBLE**

  And we know that for those who love God all things work together for good, for those who are called according to his purpose. (Romans 8:28)

- **REFLECTION**

  Where in your life do you need to ask God to rescue you today?

- **PRAYER**

  Jesus, please help me believe that if I follow you, nothing happens to me, but everything happens for me!

7

LEGACY

When the lights shut off
And it's my turn to settle down
My main concern
Promise that you will sing about me
Promise that you will sing about me

'SING ABOUT ME, I'M DYING OF THIRST'
KENDRICK LAMAR

WE WILL ALL BE REMEMBERED FOR SOMETHING

What is the legacy of Michael Jordan and Kobe Bryant? On a basketball level it is fairly simple. Off the court things can get a little more complicated. Let's dive into on-court accomplishments and cultural impact first. Both NBA legends share three undisputed legacies: sneakers, numbers and rings.

Before Michael Jordan, basketball shoes were just basketball shoes. The Air Jordan shoe was introduced November 17, 1984. Spike Lee's iconic Nike commercial in 1984 had America believing, "Money, it's gotta be the shoes!" For the past 36 years, the Air Jordan shoes have dominated popular culture. The Air Jordan has 33 separate styles and color ways. (Raise your hand in the air if you own all 33!) In 1997 the Air Jordan franchise was so big that Nike began it's own Jordan brand. In his dealings with Nike, Jordan has made roughly $1.3 billion and Nike has become one of the most valuable consumer brands in the world.

While inspiring many to work hard and pursue their basketball dreams, the shoes have been the source of robberies, assaults, murders and are to this day the first targeted products in city wide violent uprising and riots. Nike owns none of the factories where Air Jordans are produced. Nike insists they only design and market the shoes. They claim ignorance and innocence as many scandalous labor incidents, even involving children, have been reported in Thailand, China, Indonesia, and most recently Vietnam.

Kobe Bryant began his career with an Adidas shoe contract. Early Kobe fans remember the first signature shoe which many called the 'Moon Boot.' People swear that shoe weighed 20 pounds and NASA made it for astronauts. It is quite possibly the ugliest shoe ever produced by a major shoe company. In 2003 Kobe gave himself the nickname 'The Black Mamba.' The Black Mamba is the nickname of Uma Thurman's character in the 'Kill Bill' film series. The symbol that adorns all of Kobe's shoes and gear was first on the sheath of her sword.

Over the course of his career, the phrase 'Mamba Mentality' impacted Kobe and all who followed him. Bryant himself defines it as the mindset that "everything negative—pressure, challenges—is an opportunity for me to rise." During the last half of his career he mentored many of the young stars around the league into the 'Mamba Mentality.' During the post-game interview after Game 7 of the NBA finals, Kyrie Irving was asked what he was thinking about when he delivered the heart dagger three-pointer over Steph Curry to defeat the massively favored Golden State Warriors. His answer was two words: "Mamba Mentality!" During the 2020 NBA playoffs, over half of the 250 players in the Orlando bubble wore Black Mamba shoes to honor Kobe Bryant and thank him for all he did for the game.

Michael Jordan and Kobe Bryant will be remembered for their sneakers.

Michael Jordan and Kobe Bryant both wore two numbers in their careers. Jordan wore number 23 during his college career at the

University of North Carolina. But that was not his favorite number. He chose 23 because his favorite number was already worn by an upperclassman player on the Tar Heels. He continued on with 23 when he joined the Bulls. Today, the number 23 is synonymous all around the globe with Michael Jordan. Fans, young and old alike, rock the Chicago Bulls 23 jersey on every continent. Innumerable 23 tattoos have been inked on the bodies of Jordan fans. Jewelers have made small fortunes on 23 ice and bling. The great irony about the impact of Jordan's number is that 23 was not his first choice. Jordan's favorite number was 45 his first number in high school, chosen to honor his older brother Larry.

Michael Jordan returned from retirement March 19, 1995 rocking the number 45. He commented on the number change in the documentary 'The Last Dance,' "I didn't want to wear 23 because I knew my father wasn't there to watch me. I felt it was a new beginning and 45 was my first number when I was playing in high school."

Wearing number 45, Jordan led the Bulls to the Eastern Conference Semifinals against the Orlando Magic. But Jordan struggled mightily in the first game of the series. They lost Game 1 on the final possession. Nick Anderson stripped the ball from Jordan and went coast to coast for a game winning fast-break dunk. Anderson said in his post game interview, "Number 45 doesn't explode like number 23 used to. Number 45 is not number 23. I could never have done that to number 23." Jordan ran onto the court for Game 2 wearing number 23. The Bulls lost that series to Shaquille O'Neal, Penny Hardaway and the Orlando Magic. But Jordan never wore number 45 again. He went on to win three more titles in number 23.

Kobe Bryant wore numbers 8 and 24 over his twenty year career. He only played for the purple and gold but almost left to play for the Los Angeles Clippers as a free agent in 2004. In 2008, he demanded a trade from a Costco parking lot and announced that he would 'rather play on Pluto than with Smush Parker and the Lakers.' The Staples Center crowd actually booed Bryant on opening night 2008 but the jeers quickly turned to cheers when Kobe dropped 25 in the first quarter. Bryant's anger turned to joy when Mitch Kupchak somehow traded Kwame Brown, Marc Gasol and Javoris Crittenton (a man who would go on to be convicted of murder) for Pau Gasol. Kobe and The Spaniard would go on to hang two more banners in the Staples Center rafters.

As mentioned in the Foundations chapter, Bryant wore number 8 because that was the number Mike D'Antoni wore in the Italian leagues. As luck would have it, Bryant's number for his first Adidas training camp was 143. Those numbers add up to eight. Bryant broke down his attitude and why he began his career repping 8, "When I first came in at 8, I was really trying to plant my flag. I had to prove that I belonged in the NBA. I wanted to prove I was one of the best in the league. 8 symbolized nonstop energy and aggressiveness."

For the 2006-2007 season, Bryant changed his jersey to number 24. Many openly wondered if Kobe was motivated to reclaim his top spot in jersey sales, making his older jersey obsolete. For Mamba, the number symbolized a decrease in physical attributes and an increase in maturity and understanding. Number 8 represented the grueling climb to the top of the NBA mountain. Number 24 captured the view from the mountain top, with his wife and children now with him to enjoy the view.

Kobe won three NBA titles wearing number 8. He won two rings wearing number 24. He appeared in 8 All-Star games with the first number. He rocked 24 in 10 All-Star games. He scored 16,777 points rocking number 8. He scored 16,866 points wearing number 24. By any standard, the career accomplishments in only one jersey is worthy of the NBA Hall of Fame. It is incredible that Kobe put up a Hall of Fame career in both numbers. Today, the number 8 jersey and the number 24 jersey hang in the rafters of Staples Center.

In 2014, Becky, my amazing wife, had a vision to create job opportunities and bless our neighbors with delicious food. Our under-resourced neighborhood is a food desert and there are many who live in the reality of limited economic options. So she recruited our dear friend Chef Michael Martinez and got to work. 5000 Pies is a social enterprise restaurant located directly across from Cabrillo High School in West Long Beach. A few years ago the restaurant received the Long Beach Mayor's inaugural 'Best Business Awards.' Not bad to be one of 12 organizations honored from a pool of 4,800 businesses.

As I waited for my Jaguar fries, a high school student from Cabrillo High School noticed my Kobe V 'Draft Day' shoes. He was on the hoops team and he told me he loved the Black Mamba. I asked him why he thought Bryant changed his jersey from 8 to 24. My new friend said he did it to prove that he was one better than Michael Jordan. I shared with him that numbers were symbolic for Kobe and to him the number 24 represented that every one of us, regardless of race, class, religion or age, receive the same gift. Each of us are given 24 hours in a day, every day. 'Mamba Mentality' makes you ask the question "What will you do with your 24 hours today?" The young player said to me, "Dang! That blows my mind!"

Michael Jordan and Kobe Bryant will be remembered for their numbers.

Jordan and Bryant combined for 11 NBA world championships. Who can forget the exalted moments of MJ and Kobe on the top of the scorer's tables holding up their hands in total victory? Jordan's last jump shot as a Bull was the ultimate walk-off. 23 made it clear in 'The Last Dance' that he did not push on Bryon Russell. The scouting report on Russell revealed that Russell did not move his feet quickly and was susceptible to the stop and pop. When Jordan stopped hard on a dime, Russell flew by him like he was on roller skates. Who can forgot the Jazz fan's faces, screaming in horror, as Jordan's jumper kept the number of Utah Jazz NBA chips at 0?

Kobe did not shoot well in Game 7 of the Lakers-Boston 2010 NBA Finals. He was 6-24 from the field. But he got his teammates involved, played big defense, hit his free throws and pulled down 15 boards from the shooting guard position. In a big head scratcher, Kevin Garnett only had 3 rebounds in this do or die game. When Kobe stood on the top of the scorer's table and threw the five fingers in the air, it was equal relief and joy that flowed from 24's heart. He had finally moved ahead of Shaq in titles won. He was now inching ever so close to his idol and his six rings. The six banners in Chicago and the five banners in Los Angeles testify to Jordan and Bryant as two of the best to ever play the game.

Michael Jordan and Kobe Bryant will be remembered for their rings.

REBELS & FAILURES

Yes, we will all be remembered for something. It would be so easy if our legacies were only our 'One Shining Moment' highlight videos. But when we are honest with ourselves, the highs in our lives are often matched or surpassed by very deep lows. When we consider our legacies, what do we do with those events, actions and mistakes that we wish we could rewind for a do over?

The Bible is full of a word called **sin**. Our larger society mocks sin and calls it a lazy guest that won't leave from an ancient party. But as pastors, we come against this stuff all the time, and from the front line we see the profound spiritual damage that it does to those who ignore it. The Scripture teaches that sin is a natural human occurrence. Isn't it interesting that no one has to watch a YouTube instructional video to learn how to sin? It just happens because it is part of our fallen nature. And contrary to our larger culture, everyone is a sinner, not just Hitler, Hefner, Bin Laden, Weinstein and the jerk that frustrates you on social media. The Scripture teaches that everyone shares the same spiritual condition outside of Jesus. We are at once rebels and failures.

The first word for sin means to trespass. These are actions outside clearly defined boundaries by God. Rebels are people who cross the line and trespass against the will of the owner. The second word for sin involves missing a mark. These are the people who fail to reach a holiness and relationship standard. Therefore, all of us are rebels and failures. Again, there is no one who is exempt from the sin virus. We will live with the symptoms and try to manage our lives with this dark reality in our souls. Together, these two words cover the positive and the negative, active and passive, sins of commission (what we do) and sins of omission (what we fail to do). Michael Jordan is a sinful person. Kobe Bryant was a sinful person. We are sinful people. Just like you.

In no way do we wish to throw stones (or shade) at Jordan or Bryant's memory. Not only are these two men our sports heroes, but we could not imagine how we would react if we possessed their supreme talent, global fame, and unlimited wealth. We shudder to think about the choices we would have made. Instead, as pastors, we are going to use Jordan and Bryant as case studies. We cannot stress enough that we are all rebels and failures. So, with that spirit of realistic humility, we draw attention to some of the specks in Jordan and Bryant's eyes, while fully acknowledging the logs in our own.

Some of the trespasses and sins committed by our NBA legends are urban myths that have taken on a life of their own. Others are very public incidents, even argued in public court rooms. From the court and locker room, 23 and 8/24's sins add to their 'rip everyone's heart out for the win' reputations. Who can forget how Kobe blew off his teammate, Caron Butler when he first joined the Lakers? In 2004, Shaquille O'Neal was traded to Miami for Caron Butler, Lamar Odom and a couple bags of balls. A story leaked about how Butler, excited to become Kobe's teammate, got Kobe's number from a friend. He called Kobe, who immediately asked, "How did you get my number?" Kobe told him to hit him back tomorrow. Butler called him the next day. But Kobe had canceled that number earlier in the morning.

Other sins are far more devastating and destroy the lives of all involved. Michael Jordan peeled back the curtain of his intense fury to be the greatest and lorded his success over any and all who challenged it. Jordan arranged for his high school freshman basketball coach to be flown to his Hall of Fame induction speech for the sole purpose of publicly humiliating the coach. During the speech he introduced the world to the man that cut Michael Jordan from a freshman basketball team. The speech also included cringe-worthy comments he made to his children. He said he felt sorry for them because they would never live up to the standard that he had established. Jordan's insatiable drive is great on a basketball court. It is not great at the dinner table or family room for game night. Jordan never learned to turn it off. No one was surprised when Michael and Juanita Jordan filed divorced on December 27, 2006.

Kobe Bryant saw his pristine image shattered at The Lodge and Spa at Cordillera in Eagle, CO. A woman and her mother met with Eagle County detectives to report a sexual assault. After hours of interrogation the detectives believed that Kobe Bryant was guilty of rape. Bryant was arrested for suspicion of rape and false imprisonment. He was formally charged by District Attorney Mark Hulbert with one felony count of sexual assault. Kobe Bryant, the 23-year-old King of Basketball, flooded the internet because he was accused of a serious crime, not because of a game winning fadeaway. The internet exploded with Mamba's mug shot, his tired eyes staring with fear into the Eagle County sheriff's camera. If you are a Lakers fan, this was one of those 'I will never forget where I was when I heard the news moment.' This moment was right there with Magic Johnson's shocking announcement, "Because of the -- the HIV virus that I have attained, I will have to retire from the Lakers...today."

The arrest and subsequent trial preparations played out on a global theatre stage. Near the conclusion of the trial, new evidence emerged about inconsistencies in the young woman's story. She recanted a few of the details. The media was relentless and private medical records about her mental health were released. The district attorney believed Bryant was guilty and should have been tried. But on August 10, 2004 Bryant's accuser hired a lawyer and filed a civil suit against him for unspecified damages. The District Attorney was furious as this legal move was a wrecking ball to his criminal case. But she had enough and did not want to proceed. The criminal case against Kobe Bryant was officially dropped on September 1, 2004.

Kobe's attorney, Pamela Mackey, shared a statement with ESPN reporter Jim Gray, who would later be the mastermind behind LeBron James's nationally televised free-agent announcement, 'The

Decision.' The attorney wrote:

Kobe was facing life in prison for a crime he did not commit. The accuser insisted on a statement as the price for his freedom. The statement doesn't change the facts: Kobe is innocent and now he is free.

Within a year Bryant settled with his accuser for an undisclosed amount of money. Records reveal he also purchased her a home in the Denver area.

What happened in Room 35 at that luxury resort in Eagle, Colorado? God only knows. What did Kobe Bryant do with his sins and trespasses? Our dear friend John Tumminello and Kobe occasionally attended the same Catholic mass in the Newport Beach area. He said that Kobe was always locked into the service, very respectful by arriving late, sitting in the back, and leaving early to avoid any distractions for other worshippers. Kobe Bryant attended the early morning mass on January 26, 2020, a few hours before he stepped onto the helicopter that would clip the ridge of a mountain and crash.

We have never had the opportunity to pastor Kobe or Michael. But we certainly hope and pray that Kobe, before his untimely death, actively put his faith in Jesus. And we pray that Michael, who still has the gift of breathe that comes only from God, also puts his hope on the cross, of Christ. It is Jesus alone that has the authority to forgive sins.

IT IS FINISHED

Why do so many Christians have the cross dangling from their neck? Why is the cross the symbol of Christianity? Why is the Bible not the symbol of faith? Why is the dove that anointed Jesus at his baptism not the symbol of faith? Why is bread not the symbol of faith? Personally, we think a throne would make a great symbol of faith (so few in this world believe that there is a throne and there is a good, good God that sits on the throne right now)! The cross is the most unlikely of religious symbols.

And it certainly stands out in stark contrast to every other major world religion. The Hindu AUM symbol represents the universe.

The Buddhist lotus flower represents the circle of life. Islam's crescent represents progress. Judaism's star of David reflects Israel and God's chosen people. But the cross stands out in great contrast from these positive symbols. Crucifixion was the most cruel method of human execution. It was designed to generate maximum pain and punishment. The poor man who was sentenced to death by crucifixion would hang on the cross for up to five days before finally breathing his last and passing from asphyxiation. Understanding crucifixion certainly adds a new dimension of God's own suffering and empathy for sinners. We wanted to preach of how much God truly understands to our friends around the world who protested police violence chanting, 'I Can't Breathe.'

This torturous and shameful death was only assigned to murderers, armed robbers and terrorists. The Roman Empire made certain every Roman citizen was exempt from crucifixion.

In **John's Gospel**, the author stood at the foot of Jesus' cross. The God who became man and never sinned chose to endure crucifixion to save the souls of rebels and failures He came to save. He endured a kangaroo court that listened to false witnesses, stacked the jury pool, and secured an 11th hour conviction apart from due process. When the Roman governor asked Jesus to defend himself, He only said, "My Kingdom is not of this world. If my Kingdom were of this world, legions of angels would descend on the earth to fight." (John 18:36) Jesus did not say a word but allowed the men he created to punch Him, beat Him, pluck out His beard, strip Him naked, mock Him with a purple robe and a crown of thorns. The Roman lictors were trained assassins. They methodically whipped Jesus mercilessly with a cat of nine tails. This instrument was a wooden weapon with nine leather straps attached, each containing an eyelet. Each strap was filled with glass and rock fragments. Jesus was whipped 39 times. The One who demanded His **disciples** carry their own cross every day could not carry His own cross. Jesus no longer had a back. Simon the African was commanded by the Roman lictors to carry God's cross.

John records one verse that helps us have the right understanding regarding Jesus' crucifixion. The last words of Jesus from the cross set our souls on fire. These words come from the One who willingly chose to die a criminal's death for a much larger reason. His words are not an act of submission or defeat. His words are the ultimate cry of victory! These last words speak of a hope and a good future for all who follow and trust. When Jesus had received the sour wine, He said, "It is finished!" and He bowed His head and gave up His spirit (John 19:30).

Think of all of the last words Jesus could have yelled. He could have complained about the injustice of His murder. But He did not yell out, "Avenge my blood." He could have asked the Roman lictors for mercy. But He did not yell out, "Make it stop!" He said none of that. Instead, He yelled "It is finished!" The last words of His sacred life teach us that Jesus was always on mission. There was never a time when He was not preparing for this ultimate sacrifice. He did not want to die. But He did because this was the only way to justly allow rebels and failures into the presence of the Holy God. The world sees the cross as the ultimate shame. But those with eyes of faith see the ultimate victory. This is why the cross, and not something full of sunshine and smiley faces, is the symbol of God's people. When Jesus yelled "It is finished!" He declared the final plan was complete and the game was now over.

THE TURNING POINT OF A NEW CREATION

On a cosmic scale, Jesus' death and resurrection mark the ultimate turning point in human history. Jesus did not rise from the dead. Instead, He came back through death, shattering it's grip on humanity. For 40 days, Jesus walked around in His **resurrected** body. Who would have ever guessed that the same God who methodically designed creation over six days, would now burst forth with his new creation in only three days? When Jesus walked out of the tomb, He not only defeated death forever, but He gave us all hope for the new creation. Jesus is the first born of the entire next species that God is in the process of creating. We like to call this Humanity 2.0!

In Jesus' death and resurrection, no one can come against God and accuse Him of being unjust. No one can say His court is shady. No one can say He threw out the law so that sinners could go free. Because on the cross, Jesus has paid for the sins of those who put their faith in Him. Therefore, Jesus' sacrifice pays the billion dollar fine that rebels and failures owe the Kingdom of God. Rather than enduring a billion years of eternal torment in hell, Jesus alone offers sinners like us an all-access passes to God and His city forever. This is why the gospel is called 'The Good News!'

This is the legacy of God. And by faith we are invited to make His legacy our own. Malcolm Muggeridge was England's David Letterman, Jimmy Fallon, and Jimmy Kimmel. He was the most popular talk show host and social commentator in all of England. He says it best when we consider our legacies and Jesus' offer to exchange our legacy for His work on the cross.

I may, I suppose, regard myself as a relatively successful man. People occasionally stare at me in the streets, that's fame. I can fairly easily earn enough to qualify for admission to the highest slopes of the IRS, that's success. Furnished with enough money and a little fame, even the elderly, if they care to, may partake of trendy diversions, that's pleasure. It might happen once in a while that something I said or wrote was sufficiently heeded for me to persuade myself that it represented a serious impact on our time – that's fulfillment. Yet I say to you, and beg you to believe me, multiply these tiny triumphs by a million, add them all together, and they are nothing, nay, less than nothing, a positive impediment measured against one drop of that living water Jesus offers to the spiritually thirsty, irrespective of who or what they are!

What is your plan to deal with your rebellion and failures? We hope and pray that you will join us as we drink the living water. Jesus promises us eternal satisfaction. Faith in Jesus is learning to drink this invisible water every single day.

We will all be remembered for something.

Faith has it's rewards!

SOULSOUL DYNAMICS

- **BIBLE**
When Jesus had received the sour wine, he said, "It is finished," and he bowed his head and gave up his spirit. (John 19:30)

- **REFLECTION**
Have you considered Jesus and His promise to love you, forgive you, and quench your spiritual thirst forever?

- **PRAYER**
Jesus, please convict me of my sin and give me the joy of faith and forgiveness.

OUTRO

DRAFT DAY

How many brothers fell victim to the streets
Rest in peace young brother, there's a Heaven for a G
Be a lie, if I told ya that I never thought of death
My brother, we the last ones left
But life goes on

'LIFE GOES ON'
TUPAC SHAKUR

DRAFT DAY

What if Michael Jordan had played for the Dallas Mavericks? It came close to happening.

In the 1984 NBA Draft, Hakeem Olajuwon was the consensus number one pick. Portland was drafting at number two and set their heart on center Sam Bowie. The Blazers never considered Jordan because he played the same position as Clyde Drexler. This was one of the great draft fails of all time. Jordan personally held this against Drexler his whole career, and on the biggest stage mercilessly humiliated Drexler for the 1992 NBA championship.

The Chicago Bulls general manager, Rod Thorn, knew ten days before the draft they would take Jordan with the third pick. He never had a conversation with Jordan but he was close friends with Dean Smith. Thorn was given private access to watch practices, where Jordan's talent, drive and destiny were on full display. Scouts believe a more relaxed setting is often a clearer predictor of future success. Coach Smith did this mainly because he thought Chicago would be a great launching pad for Michael.

One of the Bulls owners wanted to draft Melvin Terpin. He was drafted with the sixth pick and was out of the NBA within four years. Rod Thorn and his team joked that if someone from ownership tried to enter the draft war room, they would lock the owner in the closet until the Jordan pick was in. The more Rod Thorn saw of Jordan, the more he loved him.

A few days before the draft, Thorn received a call from Rick Sund, general manager of the Dallas Mavericks. He offered to trade All-Star forward Mark Aguirre to Chicago for the third pick. Aguirre, a Chicago native, was a local hero from DePaul University. He would certainly sell tickets as Bulls attendance was at an all time low. Aguirre was himself the number one pick three years earlier. He finished the 1983 season as the second leading scorer in the league. Sund thought offering Aguirre would allow the Mavericks to draft Michael Jordan. Thorn politely passed on the offer. Reflecting on the negotiations some thirty years later, Sund praised Thorn. "Rod would have won the press conference. But the Mavericks would have won all those championships."

Although Thorn and the Bulls had fallen in love with Jordan, no one dared to dream how high he would fly. No one envisioned him becoming the greatest NBA player of all time. In the documentary 'The Last Dance,' Rod Thorn joyfully reflected on a phone call he received from one of the coaches. The Bulls were just two days into Jordan's first training camp. Practice had finished and the coach could not contain himself. Thorn said the coach was yelling into the phone, "Rod, Jordan is really, really good!"

On a personal note, we feel the same way about our amazing wives. We like to say that our far better halves, Kimberly Thomas and Becky Teter, fell to us from heaven, just as Jordan fell to the Bulls. And just like Thorn, we can barely contain our joy as we realize that our wives are really, really good!

David Stern on July 18, 1984: "With the third pick of the 1984 NBA Draft, the Chicago Bulls select Michael Jordan, from the University of North Carolina."

What if Kobe Bryant played for the New Jersey Nets? It came close to happening.

To understand Kobe's NBA draft process we must consider how Michael Jordan's global success affected the secondary business markets. Sonny Vaccaro is the famous mastermind of AAU youth basketball and the ABCD Elite basketball camps. Vaccaro worked for Adidas and was commissioned to find the next Michael Jordan. The European shoe company wanted a piece of the sweet, sweet NBA pie. Vaccaro was convinced Bryant, who he scouted at his national youth camps, was destined to be the face of Adidas basketball. Before Bryant was drafted or played one minute with the Lakers, the seventeen year-old signed a $48 million shoe contract with Adidas. The company even put his father Joe on payroll as a good will gesture. He was paid $150,000 a year to be Kobe's dad and rock the three stripes at youth tournaments.

After Bryant announced that he was taking his talents to the NBA, many franchises requested pre-draft workouts. Team Kobe turned down almost every single request. He did schedule workouts with Charlotte and Sacramento because they had early picks in the draft. But Kobe ghosted them. No call. No warning. No apology. No chance. His agent, Arn Tellem, one of the first true power brokers in the NBA, assured Bryant that it would all work out. Tellem hoped Bryant would land in LA or New York, the two biggest markets in the league.

Early in the process Tellem arranged workouts with the Nets and the Lakers. Because of their proximity to New York City, and being so close to Lower Merion, the Nets were considered a good landing spot. Kobe's workout blew away Nets general manager John Nash. The next day Kobe was scheduled for his workout with the Lakers. Tellem asked the Nets to pick up the bill for Kobe's flight to La-La Land. The Nets had no idea that Bryant would be working out for the Lakeshow. Bobby Marks, an up and coming star in the Nets front office, booked Bryant into a middle seat in coach. Tellem and the Bryant family were furious Marks did not book a first class ticket. To this day, Marks believes that the economy middle seat blunder is why Kobe never played for the Nets.

After a 45-minute workout at the Inglewood YMCA, Jerry West, general manager of the Los Angeles Lakers, told Lakers owner Jerry Buss that he would select Kobe over Allen Iverson, the undisputed number one pick in the 1996 draft. Two days later West and Tellem scheduled Bryant to play one-on-one against retired NBA defensive legend Michael Cooper. West told his former player, "Coop, make him work!" Cooper replied, "No problem, Logo!" After the workout West called Tellem and told him, "That was the single best workout I have ever seen in my life."

West tried to move heaven and earth to secure an early draft pick. He called his friend John Nash. The Nets held pick seven. He offered young center Vlade Divac. Nash immediately declined the offer, ran down the hallways to the office of young coach John Calipari and exclaimed, "Jerry West called to trade up in the draft. I know he is targeting Kobe. If West thinks he's a superstar, we are taking him!"

John Nash was a seasoned NBA general manager. John Calipari was a 37 year-old first year NBA head coach. This was his first professional draft. Joe Taub, the owner of the New Jersey Nets, did not have a clearly defined decision making structure so the three men defaulted into majority rules. Nash was sold on Bryant. Taub feared Bryant was too young. Calipari wanted to make a name for himself, and bristled at Nash's long term vision. Calipari had a guaranteed five year contract but he was insecure and wanted to prove he was big time. And did we mention that the Nets made a seventeen year old Kobe Bryant fly across America in a middle seat in coach?

On June 25, 1996, one day before the day before the draft, Arn Tellem called Coach Calipari, not Nash. He played the inexperienced coach like a piano, "If the Nets select Bryant at pick seven, Kobe will hold out and begin his professional career in Italy." Calipari ran into Nash's office to spill the tea. Nash knew Tellem was bluffing but

Calipari was scared. A few hours later, David Falk, Michael Jordan's mega-agent, who also represented a player named Kerry Kittles, called Coach Calipari, not Nash. He also threatened the inexperienced coach, "If the Nets do not select Kerry Kittles at pick seven, no one I represent will ever consider playing for the Nets." Calipari began to meltdown. For the second time, he ran into Nash's office to report they should take Kittles. The battle-tested general manager knew Tellem called up his buddy Falk to launch a coordinated attack on his inexperienced coach. The GM told Calipari to chill like EPMD, "John, they are bullying you."

On June 26, 1996, the entire New Jersey Nets leadership group ate steaks and drank wine at a posh New York City restaurant 90 minutes before the draft. Taub, Nash, and Calipari were prepared to announce to the ownership group that they would select Kobe Bryant at pick seven. But as dinner was winding down, Calipari stood up at the table to make an announcement. "If Kerry Kittles is available at pick seven, we are selecting him. If he is gone, then we will take Kobe Bryant." The ownership group loved the conviction of their shiny new coach. Everyone around the table cheered. But John Nash sank into his seat. His insecure, upstart coach had been tricked by the mega-agents and had publicly betrayed him.

As the 1996 draft was winding down, Rod Thorn approached Nash. In 1984, Rod Thorn rejected the trade offer from Dallas and drafted Michael Jordan. Earlier in the month Thorn celebrated number 4 of his 6 NBA titles. He commented to his friend, "John, Jerry West called me yesterday. I really thought you were taking Kobe Bryant."

Nash could barely conceal his pain. "So did I, Rod. F*ck! So did I."

David Stern: "With the thirteenth pick in the 1996 NBA Draft, the Charlotte Hornets select Kobe Bryant, from Lower Merion High School in Pennsylvania."

Kobe Bryant was a Charlotte Hornet for five days.

On the morning of the draft, the Lakers and Hornets agreed on a trade. The Lakers would send Vlade Divac to the Hornets for the thirteenth pick. But the trade was not announced publicly because

Vlade did not want to move to Charlotte. Three days after the draft he threatened to retire. But he eventually came around on the deal saying, "I will play in Charlotte. I will do anything to help the Lakers. They have been so good to me."

During the draft, everyone thought the deal was done and it would be announced by Commissioner Stern. Dave Cowens, the head coach of the Charlotte Hornets, sure thought the deal was done. He was assigned the task of calling Bryant a few minutes after he was drafted to tell him he was being traded to the Lakers.

Kobe Bryant said he never forgot that conversation.

"You know Kobe, it's a good thing we're trading you because we couldn't have really used you anyway," said Cowens.

"Oh, alright," said Bryant, "It's like that."

Cowens insists he was misquoted and was only talking about playing time. But Bryant shared far and wide to anyone who would listen that the hate would only fuel his own development.

The Kobe V Black Mamba signature shoe was released in 2006. For the next eleven years, until Bryant retired in 2016, each and every shoe included a Charlotte Hornets color way. It is Kobe Bryant's annual insult to Dave Cowens and the Charlotte Hornets. The white, purple and green (the color scheme of the Hornets) shoe is called 'Draft Day.'

Kobe Bryant, one of the top five players of all time, was a Charlotte Hornet for five days.

THE FATHER AND HIS LOST SON

As we mentioned in the introduction, Jesus is a master teacher and storyteller. He used stories or parables to reveal deep truths about God. He could have dropped elite level truth on people but he was all about the local neighborhood and the common people. Many think his greatest story is a father who lost his son. This story teaches us about the God who Jesus has made known:

And he said, "There was a man who had two sons. And the younger of them said to his father, 'Father, give me the share of property that is coming to me.' And he divided his property between them. Not many days later, the younger son gathered all he had and took a journey into a far country, and there he squandered his property in reckless living. And when he had spent everything, a severe famine arose in that country, and he began to be in need. So he went and hired himself out to one of the citizens of that country, who sent him into his fields to feed pigs. And he was longing to be fed with the pods that the pigs ate, and no one gave him anything.

"But when he came to himself, he said, 'How many of my father's hired servants have more than enough bread, but I perish here with hunger! I will arise and go to my father, and I will say to him, "Father, I have sinned against heaven and before you. I am no longer worthy to be called your son. Treat me as one of your hired servants."' And he arose and came to his father. But while he was still a long way off, his father saw him and felt compassion, and ran and embraced him and kissed him. And the son said to him, 'Father, I have sinned against heaven and before you. I am no longer worthy to be called your son.' But the father said to his servants, 'Bring quickly the best robe, and put it on him, and put a ring on his hand, and shoes on his feet. And bring the fattened calf and kill it, and let us eat and celebrate. For this my son was dead, and is alive again; he was lost, and is found.' And they began to celebrate. (Luke 15:11:24)

The Father has two sons. The younger son decides he doesn't want to wait until his father dies to get his inheritance. In the ultimate slap in the face, the son tells the father, "You are dead to me and I want your money." The Father gives him the bag. He goes to Vegas and is the life of the party while the money flows. But the son burns through the family fortune quick. He then finds himself alone and on the streets.

Jesus says the young man comes to his senses and comes up with a plan. The servants at his Pops' house eat well. He will return home and ask if he could become one of the servants. He knew he blew it and what he did can never be undone. And so he began the long journey home.

As he is approaching the family estate, he has no idea that the father never stopped loving him. Jesus tells us that the Father saw him while he was a long way off. That means the Father was looking for him. He likely spent every day looking down the driveway wondering if this was the day His son came home. When He finally does see his son, He cannot contain the joy. He runs to his son. He hugs his son. He kisses his son. He reinstates him as a full member of the family. He kills the fatted calf (which is only killed once in a lifetime for weddings and the most important guests of honor). The Father rejoices because His son who was lost is now found! The son He thought had died was alive!

In so many ways we are like the son. We are all rebels and failures. We are all are guilty of rejecting the Father's love and doing things our way. We've walked away, made horrible life decisions and found ourselves suffering the consequences. And if we are really honest, many of us condemn ourselves thinking we have blown our good and happy future.

But Jesus tells us this story because He wants us to know that the Father is just different. No matter what we have done, the Father runs to us, embraces up, cleans us up, and heals us in every way.

GOD IS DIFFERENT

Today in the NBA when someone is truly exceptional they are labeled as 'different.' That's why people Tweet about LeBron: "He Different." We are here to tell you the good news that God is different.

When I (PMT) was 17 years old, I was completely lost. I was gang affiliated, facing a teenage pregnancy and fatherhood. My relationships at home were broken. I was battling depression and contemplated suicide. I literally ran away from home and fended for myself on the streets, when my spiritual auntie brought me to Jesus. She brought me to a church that taught me that God is different. Every day He looked down the driveway wondering if I would be coming home that day. When He saw me, He lifted his robe and sprinted to me. Before I could even give my excuses, He covered me with love. He covered the shame of my past and mistakes and gave me a fresh start.

In Jesus, I saw that I am not the sum-total of my past and bad choices. He showed me that even today, there is enough love to forgive me, to cleanse me, and restore me to the son-ship He always had for me. This is what makes the God of the Bible 'different.' While He has every right to condemn, He loves.

Our own love runs out on ourselves. We focus on the mistakes we have made. We cannot seem to forgive ourselves for what we have done. But God is different. His love is too busy being excited that who was once lost has now been found. And the love of the Father never leaves us in the pig pen. His love cleanses us, renews us and restores our status and identity. His love, if we accept it, creates a new person. There has never been a day when this 'Different God' has not loved you.

If you are reading this book, you are hungry and thirsty for something that only comes from the Father. The world endures perpetual famine—offering us nothing that heals our souls. But because of Jesus' finishing work on the cross, He invites us home.

I encourage you, do not let your guilt or false sense of perfection get in the way of your true destiny. You can begin an authentic relationship with God today. He will forgive you. He will feed you. He will make you whole. And you can live in His paradise city for 100 billion years after you transition through the thin veil of death. This is the best contract ever offered. This is the good news of God.

May you choose God. If you are far from God, we pray you choose to come home!

HE MAKES THE DEAF HEAR

A few years ago I (JT) preached at a new church plant in Hong Kong. The church started a few months earlier and they asked me to preach their ninth service. The church is located in the Sham Shui Po district of Hong Kong. There are eighteen districts in Hong Kong and Sham Shui Po is the poorest of the poor. The church is planted across the street from a low-income government apartment complex. In America poverty spreads far and wide. But because of limited space, poverty in Hong Kong is vertical. The high rise building across the street from the church is filled with drugs and prostitution, two staples of gang related income streams.

Mr. Wong was a former leader in the Triad organized crime syndicate. He hated Christianity because his son became a Christian.

In Chinese culture it is a great insult to leave the religion of your father. But his son fell in love with Jesus and was following Him even though his family rejected Him. I don't know the details of why it happened, but Mr. and Mrs. Wong attended the eighth service. Moments before the Sunday service started, I saw them walking through the church doors. They sat in the front row. During the songs and announcements, I noticed that Mrs. Wong would speak directly (and quite loudly) into Mr. Wong's ear.

I preached from Luke's account of Jesus fishing for a fisherman (Luke 5:1-11). Like many of us, Peter was afraid that he had done too much dirt in his life. He was certain that Jesus would judge him. But Jesus tells the fishermen to not fear. He promised to forgive Peter's sins and give him a good and happy future. At the end of the message, I asked if God was speaking to anyone's heart and if they wanted to become a Christian and start following Jesus. Mr. Wong immediately raised his hand. Mrs. Wong's hand soon followed. Serving them their first communion is one of the great honors in my pastoral ministry.

In our dumpling-filled debrief after the service, I was shocked, stunned, and astonished to learn more details about Mr. Wong's life and conversion. I had no idea he was a big time Hong Kong Triad leader. And I was amazed to learn that Mr. Wong was deaf. This is why Mrs. Wong needed to speak directly into his ear during the service.

The Hong Kong pastor told our group that we were in the presence of a great sign. Mr. Wong told the pastor that when I began my sermon, he suddenly heard every single word that I spoke in English and the translator spoke in Cantonese. He said his hearing went from 0 to 10. Mr. Wong said that his deafness left him. When I asked who wanted to become a Christian, he immediately raised his hand because God broke powerfully and literally spoke into his heart and mind. Immediately when the sermon finished, his hearing went back from 10 to 0.

For the next year, Mr. Wong grew strong in his faith. He turned from evil. He cut off all gang ties. He even brought a small jackhammer to his apartment to smash out all of the idols in his life and apartment. Mr. Wong's faith spread throughout Sham Shui Po as he told many what God had done for him. Recently I learned that Mr. Wong passed away during the Covid-19 pandemic. I thank God for his life. And I cannot wait to see him again when it is my turn to walk through the valley of the shadow of death and enter into paradise.

WHEN THE END IS THE BEGINNING

We now arrive at the end. But our end is really your beginning. We trust that in reading *Jesus, Michael and Mamba* the Holy Spirit is helping you hear God call your name.

David Stern called Michael Jordan's name June 19, 1984. He rose, walked to the podium, greeted the commissioner and became a Chicago Bull.

David Stern called Kobe Bryant's name June 26, 1996. He rose, walked to the podium, greeted the commissioner, and became a Charlotte Hornet.

But we are preaching about Someone so much greater than David Stern. We are pointing you to a team so much greater than the Bulls or the Lakers.

Jesus called John Teter's name May 8, 1992. John rose, followed Jesus, and became a child of God.

Jesus called Michael Thomas' name March 13, 1994. Michael rose, followed Jesus, and became a child of God.

It is important to contrast just how different these drafts really are. Jordan and Bryant were drafted into a business. Jordan wore the Bulls jersey for fifteen years. Bryant wore the purple and gold for twenty years. Jordan ended up playing for the Wizards. NBA players always say, "Get what you can, while you can, because this is a business."

But Jesus does not draft us into a job. He drafts us into a love relationship. He would never trade you or cut you. Jordan and Bryant enjoyed twenty years of earthly glory. When Jesus calls your name, he offers you an eternal glory that will never end.

Jesus is calling your name.

Will you rise, walk to the stage, and commit your life to God?

He will not give you an NBA hat. He will give you a crown of thorns, symbolic of the hard life of discipleship.

Today is your draft day.
Please rise and walk in faith.
It will be the best decision you will ever make…

What can we say?
PMT & JT Out!

SOUL DYNAMICS

- **BIBLE**

  For this my son was dead, and is alive again; he was lost, and is found.' And they began to celebrate. (Luke 15:20-24)

- **REFLECTION**

  What is blocking you from returning home to the waiting (and running) Father?

- **PRAYER**

  Jesus, thank you for calling my name! Please help me to stand up and come home.

- **FAITH STEP**

  To begin your new life in Christ please do the following:

  1. Pray - *"Jesus, have mercy on me a sinner. I choose to follow you all of my days. Please disciple me to become a mature Christian. Please fill me with your Holy Spirit, today, and help me be your disciple for all the days of my life. I renounce the devil and his power in my life. I belong to you as I become a person of faith!"*

  2. Community - *Please reach out to any Christians that you know and share with them your amazing decision to join Jesus' team. It is really hard to follow Jesus alone. They will be excited for your faith and will help you join the team of their local church.*

  3. Training - *Please go to* **jesusmichaelmamba.com** *and check out our resources page. These tools will help you grow. Think of this site as your first training camp! Get after your faith like MJ and 'Mamba Mentality.'*

ACKNOWLEDGEMENTS

This book stands on the broad, strong and hard working shoulders of all of those who have gone before us. Jordan and Bryant are two of the brightest shining stars not only in basketball, but in all of sports. We are thankful for those who have done the deep work of interviews, reading previous books, and shaping all of the information into compelling books about Air Jordan and Black Mamba. Those who have gone before us have have made our work so much easier.

David Halberstam's classic book *Playing for Keeps: Michael Jordan and the World He Made* was our primary source for the Jordan foundation stage and his career at North Carolina. Halberstam's work is invaluable to anyone interested in Jordan and how he transformed the NBA and the business of sports.

Jeff Pearlman's *Three Ring Circus: Kobe, Shaq, Phil and the Crazy Years of the Lakers Dynasty* is such a gripping read. We actively recommend this book to all of our friends. Pearlman helped us immensely with the 2000-2004 section of Kobe's career. This balanced and fair minded journalist provides many of the stories, quotes, team dynamics, and careful analysis on Kobe's rape trial that fill this book.

The Gold Standard: Building a World Class Team is Mike Kryzyzewski's detailed account of the 2008 Redeem Team. Kobe Bryant's leadership, drive, commitment to team, and humanity are highlighted as Coach K takes us inside the run to gold at the Beijing Olympics.

Roland Lazenby's *Showboat: The Life of Kobe Bryant* provided details about Kobe's family, youth experiences and how his early years in Italy shaped who he would become.

We appreciate Phil Jackson's significant contribution of three books: *Sacred Hoops, The Last Season,* and *Eleven Rings.* Jackson's insights and quotes paint a fuller picture of Michael and Kobe. As pastors we particularly appreciated the hope Jackson's writing offers for broken relationships. It is amazing that Kobe and Phil became friends again after *The Last Season* was published. It is truly astonishing these two won two more titles together. This is a great testament to the power of reconciliation.

Carl Ellis is a bright light that shines in the dark world. His work *Free At Last* has helped us understand the gospel and better communicate the Good News to those who do not yet believe. This work is but a small application of his excellent work on core issues.

Darrell Johnson is truly one of the great Bible teachers in all the world. His book *The Story of All Stories* on the Genesis account helps us understand God, creation, sin and what it means to be a human being. The Lord has blessed Darrell as he has given his life to the careful study and passionate preaching of God's Word!

We are indebted to Jen Mallari for her 'Steph-ortless' work of detailed edits, word choice and transitions. She is such a gifted editor and helped us avoid considerable mistakes in our book.

We thank God for Cindy Kiple. Her cover and interior design are gifts from our creative God. She lived in Chicago for all of the Bulls titles and was, and still is, a big Michael Jordan fan.

And finally, thank you to Isaac Flores, Rick Cox and the entire the Los Angeles Laker Band. Section 308. 5 banners. 81. Game 7. 60. Mamba Out!

GLOSSARY

Adam and Eve - The first humans that God created. God formed them as clay and then breathed into their nostrils to make them alive. God formed them as the first family, making them partners in every way. If there were a greater gender, it is arguably woman. Eve is described as the helper implying that only Adam needed help.

Amen - The word captures the phrase 'so be it.' It is used at the end of prayers as a conclusion to communicate with God. When we say amen, we are telling God how much we need Him to answer our prayers. And we are telling Him that we believe He will answer our prayers.

Animals - God created animals to reveal an otherwise hidden part of His glorious nature. There are divine traits that we would not experience apart from the animals. Because of animals we know that God is gentle, loyal, kind and sweet. There are three heads over the earth in the Bible: Adam, Noah and Jesus. All three were surrounded by animals. The Kingdom of God, and the throne in the center, is currently surrounded by animals who worship God. This gives us a whole new perspective on God's love for us, animals and our pets.

Apostles - An apostle is a disciple of Jesus who has been given the spiritual gift to start new ministry. Church planters are people God has called and gifted to plant new churches. Every church began the same way: God inspiring men and women to begin a new church. Many church planters have the spiritual gift of apostleship.

Bible - The Bible is not just for learning, but for living. This collection of 66 books and letters is the primary source of our faith. Many call the Bible a mystery because it somehow speaks directly to us when we open it up. But it turns out the mystery is a Person. The role of the Holy Spirit is to make the text come alive and bring conviction. There are 39 Old Testament books and 27 New Testament books. There are

40 separate authors that cover a span of over 4,000 years. The authors come from every dimension of society: men, women, kings, queens, physicians, fishermen, outcasts, and even murderers. Yet all 40 authors paint a compelling and unified picture of an amazing God whose nature is set apart from every other religion and lesser god.

Bible Study Habits - There are four levels of Bible mastery: (1) Devotional - Hearing from the Word as you pray; (2) Familial - Reading the entire Bible or larger sections to learn, but not particularly study; (3) Topical - Identifying important discipleship areas to understand: family, children, money, sexuality, call, and many others; (4) Core Book Study - Deep dive and careful study of a key book or section of Scripture.

Chapter and Verse - Under the rule of King James of England (not King James of Akron, Ohio), editors were commissioned to give chapter and verse to the Biblical books. King James believed if chapter and verse were included then people could more easily memorize the Bible. For example 2 Timothy 2:5 is the letter of 2 Timothy (book 16/27 of the New Testament); the second chapter and verse 5.

Core Issues - Every one has very real needs in our lives. Core issues are foundational concepts and experiences that must be strengthened or the entire operating system is in jeopardy. Many core issues transcend race, class, and culture. Jesus promises to strengthen and resolve each and every core issue in our lives. Our book highlights seven core issues every human must address.

Daniel - As a boy he was trafficked from Jerusalem to Babylon. But he did not bow to the corrupt Babylonian culture. He and his friends were firm in their faith. God give him visions and dreams. This gave him spiritual power to preach the gospel of God to three kings. At age 73 he was arrested for his faith and thrown 12 feet down into a den of lions. But God miraculously delivered him. He is the Old Testament model of faith in a faithless world.

Darkness - Before the heavens and earth were created, everything was in a dark chaos. Darkness is not only the absence of light but the presence of evil. It is interesting that we do not need to be taught how to be evil. It is our sinful, human nature. But we do need to learn righteousness.

Deceit - The goal of the devil for each and every person is to cause humans to reject God's love, truth, gifts and salvation in our lives. He messes with our minds by feeding us 'sugar coated lies' about God. The Bible teaches that when we eat these sweet lies, we are deceived, our capacity to love God and truth shrivel, and our souls get harder and harder to God (Hebrews 3:12-13).

Demons - Spiritual beings that carry out the mission of Satan's dark army. Demons operate in military rank according to purpose, region, and experience. Demons exist to deceive, torment, and destroy faith in Jesus. They must be given permission to enter into a soul, which unfortunately, many do without even knowing it. Demons are like rats in that they go where there is trash. The best way to fight demons in our lives is to have strong faith in God, removing all of the sinful trash from our mind, soul and life.

Devil - His name is Lucifer which means 'star of the morning.' He was full of wisdom and beauty, had great power and influence in heaven, and was even called 'the guardian cherub.' But this was not enough for him because he wanted to be like God. Jesus calls him a liar, thief and murderer (John 8:44) from the very beginning. Today his mission is to destroy faith in God so that humans will join him in the eternal torment of hell.

Disciple - The first followers of Jesus were called disciples. A disciple is an apprentice and student, someone who is learning to live their lives from the teacher. We believe being a disciple of Jesus, learning to follow Him in every dimension of our lives, is the most important and smartest decision we will ever make.

Dividing Wall of Hostility - Racism is a spiritual issue. The Apostle Paul speaks of an invisible cosmic wall that is not only a barrier, but is full of active hostility. We like to think of a big wall that not only divides people, but is electric and super charged. When we run into painful, hostile and violent racist encounters, this is the evil one attacking us with his invisible weapon.

Eternity - Did you know that we live in a world that is inside another world? Eternity is the world just beyond the thin veil of our reality. If one grain of sand is equal to 80 years of life on earth, the rest of the beach is eternity. It is truly immeasurable that Jesus claims that living his Word in faith will result in a billion years in heaven. But rejecting His teachings and not choosing faith will bring about billions of years of torment and suffering.

Evangelism - The word means spreading good news. Think of someone who is friends with a billionaire offering free trips to Hawaii to the first 1,000 people. An evangelist is someone who frantically texts (like Radio One in the film 'Crazy Rich Asians') every contact in their phone to sign up before it's too late. We are evangelists sharing about the great news of Jesus. His offer is literally a billion times better than a free trip to Hawaii.

Faith - Believing God's promises and acting in a way that proves our trust in God and His Word. The best way to understand faith is to relate to Jesus as a patient does to their doctor. Jesus says, "I am the Great Physician" (Mark 2:17). In His loving care, the doctor gives us a prescription for our health. If we obey the doctor, we will enjoy the benefits of good health. If we reject the doctor, we do not believe in Him and suffer the consequences. Faith in God is obeying His commands as we deepen, heal and tell others about our spiritual Physician!

Finishing - According to the vast research of Dr. J. Robert Clinton, only 1/3 Christian leaders will finish well. 2/3 will drop out, disqualify themselves, or plateau before they complete the race God has given us to run. Many of us have been discouraged by pastors, ministers and Christian leaders who have fallen. Sadly, this is the norm. May younger Christian leaders heed the warnings.

Genesis - The first book of the Bible. The title of the book can also be translated 'Origins.' It does not scientifically calculate how the world was made. But this narrative captures God's purposes and heart in creation. Many have said that if you embrace the first four words of the Bible, your faith is off to a good start: "In the beginning God…" (Genesis 1:1).

Grace - An undeserved gift from God. The word grace is a very popular Christian word but is often under appreciated. Grace is best understood when put next to justice and mercy. Justice is sinners like you and me getting exactly what we deserve. Who wants justice? Not us! Mercy is sinners like you and me not getting what we deserve. Instead of a 20 year sentence, we are given no jail time. Grace is even better. Grace is sinners like you and me receiving what we do not deserve. Instead of a 20 year sentence in prison, grace is being gifted a beach front condo in Maui. We must choose to admit our sin to receive God's grace.

Heart - When the Bible says heart, the authors are not talking about the physical organ that pumps our blood. In the minds of the Bible authors, heart and soul are the same thing. And the soul is the spiritual command center that aligns our identity, values, and decisions. The heart is also our inner-most dwelling, where Jesus makes the stunning promise that through the Holy Spirit, He comes to live inside of us. Christians are never alone in the journey of faith. Jesus, the true God, lives inside of us as He shepherds our lives.

Heaven - There are actually two heavens. The first is what Bible scholars call 'Intermediate Heaven.' This is a next dimension paradise where God the Father, Son and Spirit and the entire host of heaven currently live. God controls all of the earth from His throne in this temporary heaven. But this is not His final home. The final heaven will be when God utterly transforms earth with glorious redemption. The city of God will come down from the sky and pour itself out over our planet, making every inch of earth holy (Revelation 21:1-22:5). This heaven will not only last for billions and billions of years, but our experience and joy of God and our new home will increase every single day.

Hell - Just as heaven is a real, physical place in another dimension, so is hell. Jesus taught extensively on hell, warning all who listen to do everything in their lives to avoid being sentenced to this spiritual prison. Those who do not put their faith in Jesus will suffer forever. Hell is described as a lake of fire that does not consume those it burns. We like to teach that hell is an ocean but instead of snorkeling and seeing fish, we suffer immeasurable pain as we inhale sulfuric fire into our lungs. But we do not die. Those who reject Jesus will live like this for billions and billions of years.

Hypocrites - There are two kinds of hypocrites. The first is the normal hypocrite. They have standards for how they should live, try and meet those standards, but fall short. That is most religious people. The other type of hypocrite is the flagrant hypocrite. They have no intention of pleasing God. Instead they do the opposite, trying to hide their sinful behavior. The pastor who sleeps around, the church secretary who steals tithes and offerings to buy a boat, and church leaders who gossip are flagrant hypocrites.

In Jesus' Name - This phrase is often used before Christian's say 'amen.' Many prayers end with both phrases. The person saying 'In Jesus' name' is saying that what they are praying and doing is in alignment with who Jesus is. In the ancient world, the name was not just identification but a description of character. So one who prays in the name of Jesus, is in alignment with the character and the person of Jesus.

Incarnation - History is full of men who would be gods, but only one God who would become a man. The word incarnation is based on

Latin's word for flesh 'carne.' To incarnate is to become flesh. John 1:14 teaches that the Word, God's Son, became flesh and literally became human. The Creator became His own creation. Every Christian is called to 'incarnate' that same love of God to those who have not yet met Jesus of Nazareth.

Jeremiah - He is the author of the Old Testament book that bears his name (29/37). He was a prophet that was appointed by God to challenge Israel to faith. The nation was at a low-point in their spiritual history, filled with darkness and disobedience to God. Jeremiah wept openly about Israel's love for sin and rejection of God. Many call him 'The Weepy Prophet.'

John - The fourth book of the New Testament was written by a fisherman named John, the Son of Zebedee. He was not only Jesus' best friend, but an eyewitness to all Jesus did and taught. He was a powerful author, penning five books and letters of the Bible. At the age of 80, he was sentenced by Caesar to a prison island for his faith. He remained strong to the very end, enduring injustice and suffering as he died alone on the prison island. The book of John is the greatest book in the history of books.

Kingdom of God - Jesus loved using this phrase to describe God's grace to bring His light into the darkness. For 2000 years, when disciples pray to God, 'Your will be done, on earth as it is in heaven' they are praying that God's Kingdom override the dark, selfish, violent and evil kingdoms of the world. The great hope of Christians is that one day our faith will become sight. We are betting our lives that one day we will experience the Kingdom of God in all of its glorious fullness.

Lay-Leader - A person who is an impactful Christian leader but does not work for the church. In large churches there are paid staff who work for the church. This is not common in small churches. The role of church leadership, however, is to not do the work of God for the church. The role of leadership is to train the congregation for

Kingdom Work. Did you know that 90% of the leaders named in the Bible were lay-leaders?

Legions - Spiritual beings (angels and demons) are organized in military ranks. There is so much more going on than meets the natural eye. Jesus speaks of legions of angels who are ready to invade Earth at his word. What a mind blowing concept that there is a unit of 6,000 angels ready and prepared for action! The New Testament also speaks of legions of demons. Jesus cast out 6,000 demons from one man (Mark 5:1-13).

Levitical Priesthood - The Old Testament records how God worked through one family, particularly through the 12 sons of Israel. His twelve boys went on to become the 12 tribes of Israel. Levi was one of these sons. The Levites were his descendants or children who God called to serve the nation of Israel as full time ministers.

Multi-Ethnic Church - Sadly, many churches today do not fulfill God's will of brothers and sisters dwelling in unity across race and class divisions. The most important church in the New Testament is the church at Antioch (Acts 11:19-30). This church was the first where Jewish and Greek disciples lived our their faith lives together. Martin Luther King preached 50 years ago that 'Sunday at 11AM is the most segregated hour in the America.' Sadly, there is still so much work to do. We must courageously follow Jesus to cross racial barriers and smash the dividing wall of hostility.

Pastor - The senior minister of a local church. This is also a verb, a spiritual gift, that helps a person get in faith from one point to another, often through an obstacle. The role of the pastor in a church is three-fold: (1) Feed the sheep with Bible teaching; (2) Develop Christian leadership; (3) Preach the gospel that those who do not know Jesus might come to saving faith.

Paul - From his early age, this Hebrew was groomed and destined for the highest levels of Jewish religious leadership. He was gifted, trained, passionate and personally mentored by the best. But this all changed when he met Jesus. He was on his way to persecute and imprison all Christians when Jesus spoke to Him as a Shining Light. His life was turned upside down in an instant.

Preaching - Men and women called by God to open, encourage, and teach the Word of God. The Word of God is living, and it does at least three things whenever it is preached: (1) The Word informs; (2) The Word of God performs; (3) The Word of God brings conviction that leads to repentance.

Prophecy - The spiritual gift of prophecy is one of the 19 gifts described in the New Testament. A prophecy is a clear message from God that the hearer would otherwise not know. Prophecies are often predictions of what God will do in the future. It often contains private information that is hidden to the one delivering the message. But the audience knows and normally responds with awe and astonishment.

Prophet - A prophet is a man or woman who God calls to deliver an otherwise hidden message from the Living God. The audience is often disciples who need encouragement and correction. God also uses prophets to warn the larger unbelieving culture. Many of the prophets from the Bible are called at a very young age. They personally experience God's awesome and life changing presence first. Then they go on to public ministry much later in their lives. A mature prophet is usually full of wisdom and empathy.

Repentance - The word repent is one of the best words in the Bible. To repent does not primarily mean to be sorrowful. It means to go another direction. If am walking to answer a phone call, but decide not to pick up the phone and walk the other direction, I have repented from the phone call. Jesus' first sermon is a clear call to repent (turn the other way from the world) and believe in the good news of God's grace (Mark 1:15).

Refining Fire - The Bible loves to use the image of fire. When the presence of God appears in our lives, the fire of faith burns away all dross, imperfections, and blemishes. The fire is not meant as a punishment but as the tool to bring true spiritual character and growth. Sadly, many disciples hang their heads when the fire begins to burn in their lives, and give up. However, wise disciples understand that this is the process of God cleaning and strengthening our faith. These disciples patiently endure the fire and go deeper into their love relationship with God.

Rescued - The book of Psalms is the songbook of the Bible. There are 150 songs recorded that declare the saving nature of God. One of the main themes of the Psalms is that God rescues sinners. To be rescued means that one is in danger. Psalm 18 paints the graphic picture of someone drowning in the ocean because strong sea creatures are dragging the person down to a certain death. But God hears the cries from heaven and personally delivers the drowning human to shore. Being rescued by God is the dominant faith theme for many Christians.

Resurrection - Jesus rose again after spending three days in the grave. This event is called the resurrection. The word resurrection is best understood when put next to the word resuscitation. To be resuscitated means to be brought back to life. A drowning swimmer is resuscitated because someone breathes air back into their lungs. But when they come back they are still a human swimmer. To be resurrected means to be re-created into an entirely new form of life. Jesus did not come back from the dead, he came back through death itself. This event shattered death's hold on the old creation. When Jesus left the tomb, He was the first born of an entirely new order of creation. Those who follow, trust and love Jesus will experience the resurrection and become part of Humanity 2.0!

Sin - An attitude or action that breaks the divine law of God. C.S. Lewis taught people about sin using the example of children waiting in line for an ice cream cone. At the earliest age, a child knows another child jumping in line in front of them is wrong. Why? Because there is an internal moral law inside each of us. Where does this come from? The internal moral law is the greatest evidence that there is a moral Law Giver. Sin is action or attitude that offends God by breaking His spiritual laws.

Sunday Best - Churches come in all shapes and sizes. Some are more traditional than others. What one wears to church can often be a point of emphasis for older churches. We must remember that Jesus teaches that it does not matter where you worship (or what you wear). The focus is that our worship must be full of spirit and truth (John 4:23). Of course, there are certainly services and special moments that demand our best so we must dress appropriately and worship on point.

Teacher - The spiritual gift of teaching is one of the 19 gifts described in the New Testament. The teacher studies the Word of God and then delivers the truth. The mark of the spiritual gift in operation is the Word being taught with a clarity that results in conviction and repentance.

Throne - Revelation, the last book of Bible, teaches us that there is a throne. The throne is the headquarters and central command of the universe. Every media outlet today reports nothing on this throne because they simply do not know. But those who have eyes to see and ears to hear know that there is a throne and the One who sits on it is full of love, grace, and authority.

Translation - There are more than a handful of translations of the Bible. The reason for this is that over the course of history many have interpreted the truth of the Biblical text for their country, community, and church. Each offer its own strengths and weaknesses. The English Standard Version of the Bible is the translation used for *Jesus, Michael & Mamba*.